The American History Series

SERIES EDITORS

John Hope Franklin, *Duke University*

Abraham S. Eisenstadt, *Brooklyn College*

R. Kent Newmyer
UNIVERSITY OF CONNECTICUT

The Supreme Court under Marshall and Taney

HARLAN DAVIDSON, INC.
WHEELING, ILLINOIS 60090-6000

Library of Congress Cataloging-in-Publication Data

Newmyer, R. Kent.
    The Supreme Court under Marshall and Taney.

    (The American history series)
    Bibliography: p.
    Includes index.
    1. United States. Supreme Court—History. 2. Marshall, John,
1775–1835. 3. Taney, Roger Brooke, 1777–1864. I. Title. II. Series:
American history series (Harlan Davidson, Inc.)
        KF8742.N49   1986   347.73'26'09   86-47549
        ISBN 0-88295-746-5 (pbk.)   347.3073509

Acknowledgments: My thanks to Maurice Baxter for his valuable
criticism, to Jackson King, Jr., for preparing tables, and to The
University of Connecticut Research Council for financial support.
Special thanks to Mrs. Darryl Kestler for her valuable editorial
assistance. For any shortcomings the book may have, I take full
responsibility.

To Jody, who helped me most of all, I dedicate the book.

Cover design: Roger Eggers Cover illustration: Culver Pictures, Inc.

Manufactured in the United States of America
00 15 MG

EDITORS' FOREWORD

Every generation writes its own history, for the reason that it sees the past in the foreshortened perspective of its own experience. This has certainly been true of the writing of American history. The practical aim of our historiography is to offer us a more certain sense of where we are going by helping us understand the road we took in getting where we are. If the substance and nature of our historical writing is changing, it is precisely because our own generation is redefining its direction, much as the generations that preceded us redefined theirs. We are seeking a newer direction, because we are facing new problems, changing our values and premises, and shaping new institutions to meet new needs. Thus, the vitality of the present inspires the vitality of our writing about our past. Today's scholars are hard at work reconsidering every major field of our history: its politics, diplomacy, economy, society, mores, values, sexuality, and status, ethnic, and race relations. No less significantly, our scholars are using newer modes of investigation to probe the ever-expanding domain of the American past.

Our aim, in this American History Series, is to offer the reader a survey of what scholars are saying about the central themes and issues of American history. To present these themes and issues, we have invited scholars who have made notable contributions to the respective fields in which they are writing. Each volume offers the reader a sufficient factual and narrative account for perceiving the larger dimensions of its particular subject. Addressing their respective themes, our authors have undertaken, moreover, to present the conclusions derived by the principal writers on these themes. Beyond that, the authors present their own conclusions about those aspects of their respective subjects that have been matters of difference and controversy. In effect, they have written not only about where the subject stands in today's historiography but also about where they stand on their subject. Each volume closes with an extensive critical essay on the writings of the major authorities on its particular theme.

The books in this series are designed for use in both basic and advanced courses in American history. Such a series has a particular utility in times such as these, when the traditional format of our American history courses is being altered to accommodate a greater diversity of texts and reading materials. The series offers a number of distinct advantages. It extends and deepens the dimensions of course work in American history. In proceeding beyond the confines of the traditional textbook, it makes clear that the study of our past is, more than the student might otherwise infer, at once complex, sophisticated, and profound. It presents American history as a subject of continuing vitality and fresh investigation. The work of experts in their respective fields, it opens up to the student the rich findings of historical inquiry. It invites the student to join, in major fields of research, the many groups of scholars who are pondering anew the central themes and problems of our past. It challenges the student to participate actively in exploring American history and to collaborate in the creative and rigorous adventure of seeking out its wider reaches.

John Hope Franklin

Abraham S. Eisenstadt

CONTENTS

We are under a Constitution, but the Constitution is what the judges say it is. . . .

CHARLES EVANS HUGHES (1907)

ONE

The Framework of Judicial Statesmanship

The Supreme Court under Chief Justices Marshall and Taney, from 1801 to 1864, spanned the formative years of the republic. During this period the American people cast off the institutional and psychological vestiges of colonial status and established the political and economic foundations, the intellectual assumptions, and the social priorities that would carry the nation into the modern age. In this enterprise of nation building the Court played a leading role. Not only did it shape the contours of national policy, but, in the process, defined its own powers and established the ground rules for judicial government. Of course, the Court's creative influence can be exaggerated. The American experience shaped the Court as much as the Court shaped the nation. No doubt the American people would have survived and the nation prospered without judicial guidance. Yet, just as certainly, the nation and the people would have been different. Something basic and unique—some would say characteristically American—would be gone. What the student of history is obliged to do, then, is to understand the special nature of judicial statesmanship, to single out and evaluate the distinctive mark it left on national history. The quest logically begins with the special qualities of judicial power —its sources, its limitations and potential.

At the very beginning of the inquiry into judicial power, one encounters ambiguity and conflict. For the fact is that the American people have never been, and are not now, entirely comfortable about the Supreme Court's policy-making role. A quasi-aristocratic institution not answerable directly to the people troubles the democratic conscience. And the fact that judicial review—the power to negate congressional acts which conflict with the Constitution and to overrule acts of state legislatures at variance with either the Constitution or federal laws—is not explicitly given in the Constitution increases these doubts. Not surprisingly, besides attacking particular decisions, the Court's critics have consistently charged the Court with usurpation and challenged the legitimacy of judicial authority itself. Their allegations require a reply.

Even the most dogged critics have to admit that the Supreme Court is no ordinary court of law. It is clear from the Constitution that the Court was intended to perform a central function in the governing process. Article III established the federal judiciary as a separate and equal branch of government with "one Supreme Court" at its head. As the direct creation of the sovereign people in convention, the Court's democratic credentials were impeccable. Unlike the high judicial courts of England and the Continent which had developed as adjuncts of the King's administrative household, the authority of the Supreme Court was on a par with the executive and the legislature. Life tenure for the judges guarded against the encroachment of the other branches and even against the momentary vindictiveness of the people themselves.

The grant of power to the judiciary—"altogether unprecedented in a free country," a contemporary observed—attests to its extraordinary character. Article III conferred two categories of judicial power. The first was based on subject matter and extended generally to all cases in law and equity arising under the Constitution, federal laws and treaties, and to all cases of admiralty and maritime jurisdiction; the second, based on the nature of the parties in litigation, covered controversies between citizen and citizen (providing they were from different states), between a state and a citizen of another state, between state and state, and state and nation. Jurisdiction in both categories puts the Court at the nerve center of public power and enables it to shape the political, economic, and social issues which depend on that power.

Yet the fact remains that judicial review, the foundation of the Court's power, was neither positively given in the Constitution nor explicated in the debates which took place at Philadelphia and at the ratifying conventions. The effort to resolve this ambiguous silence on the legitimacy of judicial review has been a major theme in the history and historiography of the Court, a theme which Alan Westin discusses in his introduction to a 1962 edition of Charles Beard's *The Supreme Court and the Constitution* (first published in 1912).* The climax of scholarly confusion came when Beard and Edward Corwin, two giants in the field, arrived at opposite conclusions after examining the same sources. Judicial review, a potential curb on democratization, fit neatly into Beard's view of the Constitution as a self-interested product of an economic and politically conservative elite; he concluded it had been the intention of the Framers to give the Court this power of review.

* For the full citation of this and other books and articles mentioned in the text, see the bibliographical essay, pages 153–66.

But Corwin insisted that although the Court frequently assumed a conservative role, it did so in response to circumstances after 1787 rather than from a constitutional mandate.

Without denying the impact of subsequent events—or Marshall's creative rendering of them—on the timing and character of judicial review, there is good reason for accepting Beard's argument that the men who drew up the Constitution had envisaged a form of "judicial control" similar to what actually developed. The most conclusive evidence for such a view comes from the wording and logic of the Constitution itself. Article VI establishes a hierarchy of law. The Constitution is the "supreme law of the land," and immediately beneath it are federal laws made "in pursuance thereof," a phrase suggesting that federal laws *not* in conformance with the Constitution are invalid. Beneath both in order of authority are state constitutions and state legislative acts. Article VI also binds state judges to this order of authority, "the Constitution or laws of any state to the contrary notwithstanding," leaving little doubt that state law must give way to the supreme law.

Taken together, Articles III and VI support the conclusion that the Court has the power to review statutes, including acts of Congress. Article III, as we have seen, establishes an independent Court and imposes on it the duty of deciding between parties who claim rights under one or another of the various strata of law. If these laws conflict, the Court must give precedence to the law which Article VI makes controlling. Section 25 of the Judiciary Act of 1789, passed by a Congress containing forty-four members who had taken part in either the Constitutional or state ratifying conventions, makes it clear that acts of Congress were included in this imperative. This clause gives the Court the power to reverse or affirm judgments, brought by writ of error from state courts, which are adverse to the validity of an act of Congress. If the Court affirms a state court decision which invalidates a congressional act, the Court is declaring that act unconstitutional.

The logic of Articles III and VI is even more convincing when viewed against the intellectual and institutional background of the eighteenth century. No doctrine was more influential in that age of constitution-making than that of a higher law—the belief in eternal, unchanging principles of right, knowable to man and binding on his actions. Since the seventeenth century, Americans had struggled to give institutional expression to this ancient doctrine in their legal codes and instruments of government. The American Revolution climaxed and formalized this quest for government under law. The supremacy clause of the Constitution translated revolutionary theory into institutional reality by identifying higher law with a written constitution. American constitutional government, shaped by legal-minded pragmatists with a stake in society and a consequent appreciation of order and stability, was, in the apt words of William Vans Murray, a government "of definition and not of trust and discretion."

Constitutional limitations, as the convention understood, required specific means of enforcement, and English and American experience pointed toward judicial review as that means. English common law had very early been identified with the higher law. And in Dr. Bonham's case (1610), Sir Edward Coke, Chief Justice of the King's Bench, invalidated an Act of Parliament authorizing the College of Physicians to issue licenses to practice medicine, implying that the judicial courts were guardians of the supreme law. His justification was that the ancient principles of common law set limits to legislative and executive powers which the common law courts were supposed to enforce. Americans accepted Coke's doctrine even though the British didn't. On several occasions before 1787, American state courts invalidated legislative acts violating state constitutions—though the power to do so was nowhere explicitly granted. The delegates at Philadelphia, who knew their history and law (thirty-four of them were lawyers), were aware of both the common law tradition and the specific state precedents. They could hardly have missed the appropriateness of judicial review as the means of enforcing limited government.

In the absence of conclusive evidence, the debate over the source of judicial review will undoubtedly continue. But even assuming, as many historians today do, that the constitutional Framers planned judicial review, we still have not determined what judicial review meant to them. When was the power to be used? What were its limits? Were the Court's decisions final and binding on the other branches of government? If the decisions were obligatory, how could they be enforced if Congress and the President were hostile to them? And the greatest uncertainty of all: Would the American people tolerate the anomaly of judicial government as they moved toward popular democracy?

After 180 years (as Wallace Mendelson, ed., *The Supreme Court: Law and Discretion,* 1967, makes clear), these questions are still unresolved. The various answers have depended and will continue to depend on the wisdom and informed judgment of the American people and, most of all, on the ability of the Court to govern wisely. For the crucial fact is that, whatever the source, the Court quickly claimed the power to govern and put it to use. And if the people are to judge the judges, it is imperative that they understand the peculiar limitations and special potential of judicial government, as well as the unique qualities of statesmanship that are called for. First, the matter of limitations.

LIMITATIONS ON JUDICIAL LAWMAKING

One thing at least is certain about the Court's powers. Though they are political, they are not simply political; while capable of shaping policy, the Court's powers differ substantially from those of Congress and the executive. For although it behaves politically by making policy, the Court proceeds by judicial means. In the last analysis, of course, its work merges with that of other branches of government. But the atmosphere of the courtroom is not that of the legislative chamber or the White House. As a judicial body the Court moves by its own particular institutional and intellectual processes and performs a specialized function in lawmaking and social change. Put simply, there are many things it cannot do.

The "most significant and least comprehended limitation" on judicial power, says Justice Robert Jackson, is that it proceeds solely on the basis of litigation. When the Constitutional Convention refused to bestow a general veto power on the judiciary by making it part of a council of revision, when it defined judicial power in terms of "cases" and "controversies," it left no doubt about the matter. That the Court can speak only when confronted by "real, earnest, and vital controversies" between parties is a substantial restriction. Since issues come before the Court only when initiated by a party to a controversy, the Court has little positive control over the timing of its decisions. Moreover, the factual environment within which the Court must make its decision, and which, as Frankfurter reminds us, determines "the extent of its sway," is usually created by a collision of parties beyond judicial control. The Judiciary Act of 1925, which gives the Court wide discretion in the selection of the cases it hears through certiorari procedure, has helped the modern Court circumvent this limitation by allowing it to choose cases that have lawmaking significance. But in the era of Marshall and Taney the great majority of cases decided—which the Court had been obliged to hear—contained little potential for shaping either law or policy.

The Court's work is conditioned not only by the nature of the cases before it but by the lawyers who argue them. The lawyer is the nexus between the citizen and the law. His brief and argument bring the facts of the case and the principles of law to be sustained by them before the Court. His skill and learning, insight and integrity, therefore, shape the work of the Court as well as the law it makes. So indirectly do the lawyer's professional connections. For the kind of social, economic, and political issues that come before the Court depend on the availability of lawyers to various groups and individuals in society. And those with power and money have generally monopolized the legal profession and, through it, have had special access to judicial power. The American Civil Liberties Union and the National Association for the Advancement of Colored People have given the poor and anonymous a new voice. But in the days of Marshall and Taney interest group litigation was still limited to privileged groups like the New England Mississippi Land Company or the privately controlled Second Bank of the

United States, and thus did not alter the private and exclusivist tendencies of the judicial process.

It is a striking fact of American history that during this period most of the great questions of public law affecting the life of the nation were framed for the Court by lawyers acting for private individuals and groups. Even in the great formative cases, the government was not represented. To be sure, the government's lawyers could bring suits to enforce national law and could appear before the Court when the United States was a party of record. But during most of the period, the Attorney General's office—the government's legal arm—was a narrowly conceived one-man operation. Until 1853, attorney generals maintained a private practice and appeared for private litigants in such leading cases as *Dartmouth College* v. *Woodward* (1819), *Cohens* v. *Virginia* (1821), *Brown* v. *Maryland* (1827), and *Luther* v. *Borden* (1849). On the other hand, counsel for the government appeared in none of the great commerce cases of the period, though litigation over the commerce clause played a key role in shaping the constitutional structure of the federal system. A department of justice was not created until 1870, and not until 1937 did the government gain the general right to become a party in suits where the constitutionality of an act of Congress was questioned. Lawyers could, of course, serve the public welfare while serving private interests. But there was no assurance that they would.

The litigious character of the judicial process places still another basic limitation on the Court. In settling authentic disputes between parties, the Court, more than any agency of government, makes law real to the people. If that law is to have authority, it must be known and respected by the community: to be known it must be consistent and clear; to be respected it must reflect the changing needs of the people. In the rule of *stare decisis* the common law had developed a method of striking the vital balance between stability and change. *Stare decisis* obliges the judge to respect principles of law established in previous decisions and apply them in all cases where the facts permit. Changed circumstances are accommodated as far as possible through extrapolation from accumulated principles. Of course, constitutional law is not the common law, and the Supreme Court is not a common law tribunal. But, for lack of its own jurisprudential system and because the justices were trained in the common law tradition, the Court adopted large portions of the methodological and philosophical premises of the common law. These self-imposed rules restrain the judge's natural inclination to read his own policy preferences into a decision.

The Court can escape from the limitations of case-controversy. But when it does, it encounters another barrier imposed by its special relation to Congress and the executive. For, despite the separation of powers principle, the Court is dependent on the coordinate branches in the performance of its duties and is vulnerable to occasional vindictiveness from them. In the first place, justices owe their appointments to the President with the advice and consent of the Senate. Life tenure frees the justice from any subsequent dependence on the President, but Presidents from Washington on have used their appointive power to influence the Court and to shape constitutional law. And more important yet, the Court relies on the executive branch for the enforcement of its decisions. Since parties in litigation are frequently sovereign states, the need for executive support is vital. Even with that support, it might be added, the effect of the Court's decisions may be delayed or dissipated either by diversionary legal tactics or by confusion in the lower courts and among the people as to their meaning. The problem was acute in the time of Marshall and Taney, when communication between the Supreme Court, the state courts, and lower federal courts was slow, when the Attorney General's office consisted, for much of the period, of one man and a few harrassed clerks, and when the standards of the legal profession were low.

The Court is even less independent of Congress. The House of Representatives can impeach judges, and the Senate can try them for treason, bribery, high crimes, or misdemeanors. In certain instances, legislators can have the last word simply by legislating around the Court's decision or by initiating amendments to undo it. Also, by packing the Court or by reducing its numbers, Congress can influence or impede the Court's work. But, most important of all, a vital portion of the Court's jurisdiction is at the mercy of Congress. With the exception of the constitutional grant of original jurisdiction—cases "affecting ambassadors, other public ministers and consuls and those in which a state shall be a party"—all other cases come to the Court by way of appellate jurisdiction "with such exceptions and under such regulations as the Congress shall make." The congressional power to structure the whole system of lower federal courts is an ever present reminder to the Supreme Court to restrain itself.

After the Court deals with these areas of vulnerability, it still has to answer to the people. Rarely does the Court defer explicitly to public opinion, but it cannot ignore the fact that, as De Tocqueville observed, it "would be impotent against popular neglect or contempt of the law." The people limit the law—and thus the Court—as an instrument of social change in a more profound way than by opposing it: they live outside it. Law is only the framework within which human activity goes on. It is no substitute for the human impulse toward creative change and social innovation. However sagacious the Court might be, it cannot make a people great or save a people bent on destruction. Individual strife calls the Court and the law into action and sets the outside limits of what they can do.

THE POTENTIAL OF JUDICIAL STATESMANSHIP

Distinct and limited the Court may be; weak in the potential of positive statesmanship it decidedly is not. Limitations on the judicial process may be overcome, and, in the hands of masters, the Court's "great and stately jurisdiction" may be translated into a constructive instrument of political, economic, and social policy.

The Constitution itself invites the Supreme Court to be more than a mere court of law. Judicial interpretation always involves discretion, since the generality of law can never encompass the particularity of life. With constitutional interpretation this is especially true. The Framers of the Constitution intended their work to govern a growing republic, so they drew up only a skeletal framework for American law, an anatomical rather than a physiological structure, Justice Frankfurter called it. Besides, since they were not omniscient, they unintentionally left gaps and uncertainties. Where the document was general, obscure, or silent, the Court has spoken up. Not everything, of course, was unsettled. But in the crucial areas, there was much play. Neither the text of the Constitution nor the debates of the Framers and ratifiers, for example, clearly defined Congress' power "to regulate commerce" or "to make all laws" which shall be "necessary and proper" for the execution of the enumerated powers. As the nation grimly discovered, congressional power to "make all needful rules and regulations" respecting territories was exceedingly obscure. So was Article I, Section 10, which prohibited the states from "impairing the obligation of contracts," and also the Tenth Amendment, which reserved to them those powers not delegated to the United States. Such vital matters as corporations, railroads, banks, and political parties were not even mentioned, though they had to be incorporated into the constitutional system. Obligated to make the Constitution a document to live by and faced with the vagaries and silences of the text, the judges fell back on, in Holmes's famous words, "the felt necessities of the time, the prevalent moral and political theories, intuitions of public policy."

The Court can make its mark on policy in less exciting areas of litigation than constitutional construction. The interpretation of federal statutes, for example, has been a vital and constantly growing part of the Court's work. Congressional legislation is complex and frequently ambiguous; the Court joins in the legislative process by performing the necessary task of filling in the gaps. Cases coming under its admiralty and maritime jurisdiction, especially in the first quarter of the nineteenth century, permitted the Court to consult the ancient and elaborate body of maritime law for rules to guide American commerce. Common law questions also consumed a large portion of judicial energy in the early years and continued to do so until the Court gained control over the cases it heard. There was, to be sure, no federal common law per se. But all the American states (except Louisiana, whose tradition was French) had the common law of England as a legal foundation, and its principles, method, and spirit permeated the whole structure of national law. The judges encountered common law questions at every turn, and the problem of selecting principles from the English inheritance that fit American circumstances provided an opportunity for shaping and forming American jurisprudence. For some, like Justice Joseph Story, it was a creative enterprise.

It should not, of course, be imagined that the business of interpreting federal law is open-ended, that the judges are unassisted or free to follow their whims. Congressional statutes frequently allow little interpretive leeway, and when the Constitution speaks clearly the Court must follow. And even when statutes are vague and the Constitution ambiguous, judicial improvisation is restrained by judicial method. In its interpretation of statutes the Court is obliged, by its own axioms of construction, to consult legislative history and supplementary legislation to clear up uncertainty. As for the Constitution, many of its phrases are already conditioned by congressional and executive action or shaped by common law usage which, since Marshall, has been a recognized interpretive guide. And once constitutional or statutory questions have been clarified by decision, interpretive latitude, if not checked, is at least partially restricted.

But none of these restraints have eliminated that element of judicial discretion so essential to the Court's statesmanship. Issues of national law, arising under a unique federal system, were frequently not amenable to common law construction. The Court need not defer to the constitutional interpretations of the other branches. Neither in fact did *stare decisis* seriously curtail interpretive latitude. Public law was born with the nation, and for many years the Court made precedents instead of relying on them. Moreover, as the Taney Court demonstrated, once made, these decisions too were subject to interpretation. In the face of changing historical demands, precedents could be and were abandoned—reluctantly to be sure, silently if possible. Such an abandonment generally weakened the obligation of *stare decisis* and, if done *sub silentio,* gave future courts a choice between two conflicting interpretations on the same point, which is to say, left them bound by no clear precedent at all.

Both the intent of the Framers and the history of the period provided the Court with interpretive guidelines and aided in the search for constitutional meaning, but neither was unduly confining. Though intent became a standard axiom of interpretation under Marshall, it remained extremely amorphous. The Constitutional Convention was secret; the delegates pledged themselves to silence and kept their word. The "official" *Journal* was not published until 1819, and it was so spare as to offer little notion of what had actually gone on. Robert Yates' account, published in 1821, and the other fragmentary personal recollections did little more to lift the veil. Not until 1840, after many of the formative constitutional decisions (based, ironically, on intent) had been made, were Madison's authoritative notes of the *Debates* published. And even they left much in doubt. The *Federalist* was available and heavily consulted, but, however profound, it was less an impartial exposition of intent than propaganda advocating ratification.

History was notoriously permissive, too, allowing the Court wide margin for interpretation. It was especially vague on the fundamental question of whether the Constitution was a source of power or an instrument of limitation. The doctrines of higher law and limited government were, as we have seen, part of the historical climate of opinion. Having waged a war against the unlimited authority of Parliament and the King, Americans had no intention of conceding the same powers to Congress and the President, and the Constitution made this clear. But the Constitution had another historical dimension. It was drawn up and ratified to correct the almost fatal lack of national power in the Articles of Confederation, to supply adequate national authority to a growing and ambitious republic. Historically, then, the Constitution was as much an instrument of power as it was of limitation. Which interpretation to choose and when were matters for judicial discretion.

And the way the Court gives its interpretation is as important as the interpretation itself and its timing. For judicial statesmanship is not simply saying yes or no to requests for power. In answering those requests, the Court adds a "reasoned justification" for its decisions. In this process of exegesis, the Court provides the people with a rational basis for understanding and obeying the law by putting it in the context of their past experience, immediate needs, and future expectations. The cumulative effect is to educate society in its own dominant social values. The Court's structure and procedures are ideal for this intellectual and educational function. Never composed of more than ten or less than six (nine since 1869), the Court is neither too small to preclude an enlightening clash of opinion nor too large to stifle debate or prevent agreement. Its internal rules permit, indeed demand, careful independent research and creative individual reasoning. The science of jurisprudence lays down the intellectual rules of the game. The responsibility of meting out justice to real people restrains careless speculation. Secrecy of conference deliberations and life tenure guarantee that the Court will be free from immediate public pressure. And the ultimate publication of the opinions induces responsibility and encourages excellence of workmanship. The opportunities for dissent and separate concurrence tend to sharpen self-criticism and foster that prescience which pioneers legal change. Probably no other agency of government, even the executive, has as much opportunity and is better constituted to speak to the rational and moral side of the American character.

It is true that the Court is restrained in the exercise of its powers both by governmental checks and balances and by public opinion. But these restraints do not always restrain. National government operates quite as much through the mutual cooperation of the separate branches as it does through their mutual suspicions and jealousies. Though it rarely makes the headlines, the Court has often worked in harmony with its coordinate branches. And not infrequently it takes interpretive clues from them. As for the Court and the people, there is much to put them at odds—the Court's nonelective membership, its secrecy, its mysterious methods, its frequently obscure language. In addition, the Court is sometimes unmistakably anti-majoritarian. But for all this, there is a possibility of intimacy between the people and the Court which enhances its authority. More than the legislative and executive branches, the Court brings the power and moral authority of the government to bear directly and often dramatically on individuals and groups. Of all the branches, it is most closely identified with the Constitution, and so popular reverence for that sacred American document accrues vicariously to the Court (as President Roosevelt discovered in 1937). Most important, however, is the fact that, in adjudicating the problems of the nation, the Court may speak for, not against, the majority. When it chooses to represent the popular will, or when it takes for the foundation of its law the highest morality of the people, it gains sufficient prerogative to carry it through the occasional transgressions on its own limitations.

THE COURT AND THE MEN ON IT

The Court is an institution and as such its structure, functions, and power may be analyzed abstractly. But it must not be assumed that the Court itself is an abstraction. As Justice Frankfurter reminds us, "individuals, with all their diversities of endowment, experience, and outlook, determine its actions." Since humanity cannot be kept from the hallowed temple, it behooves us to ask what human qualities are in demand there —what qualities make judicial statesmen of justices.

To begin with, a justice must have a mastery of the law and a deep knowledge of the workings of society. And more. The narrow, often selfish, interests of parties before the Court must be understood in relation to history, must be projected into the future, and measured against the general welfare. That understanding, translated into legal precept, must then be brought coherently and clearly, and eloquently if possible, to the printed page. It is work for thinkers and—as Justices Holmes, Cardozo, and Frankfurter demonstrate—for the historian, philosopher, prophet, and poet. All these the great judge must be without ceasing to be a judge, that is to say, without ceasing to strive for the ideal of law—the regular, rational, and impartial administration of justice.

Few justices have possessed these high qualifications in sufficient degree to be called judicial statesmen. On the other hand, there were few who did not possess enough of these qualifications to make an honest contribution to the work of the Court. Even the great justices rarely possessed all of them or applied them with perfect consistency. And each man, small or great, has had to pit his qualities of judicial greatness against his human foibles. Thomas Reed Powell makes the point well:

. . . Judges may have passions and prejudices as do men of lesser breed without the law. Judges argue from undisclosed assumptions, as may you and I. . . . They form their judgments after the varying fashions in which you and I form ours. They have hands, organs, dimensions, senses, affections, passions. They are warmed and cooled by the same summer and winter and by the same ideas as a layman is.

From the unavoidable intrusion of this humanity into the business of judging comes the final qualification for greatness. Oliver Wendell Holmes expressed it succinctly: Asked by a friend what his secret was, he replied simply, "Long ago I decided that I was not God." From this admission might come, as it did in Holmes' case, a skepticism about absolutes, a self-imposed judicial restraint, and a realization that the Court frequently governs best when it governs least.

Though individuals make up the Court, eventually the student of history must return to a consideration of the Court as an institution, to its collective nature. For here the whole is truly greater than the sum of its parts. It is the opinion of the Court—the product of the private interchange of ideas among the several justices, the collective reasoning of the judicial conference—that becomes law. It almost always embodies ideas from previous conferences, from earlier opinions, indeed, from the entire historical experience of the Court. Excessive individuality, moreover, is softened by institutional responsibilities and checked by a sense of tradition and collective destiny. Brilliance of mind and artistry of expression are called forth by circumstance, to be sure. But even such instances of genius lean on the body of the whole Court and the ancient tradition of the law.

The complexity of judicial creativity and the difficulty of the Court's task should caution the historian against snap judgments or simplistic interpretations. Forewarned, then, and with a notion of what it can and can't do, let us consider how the Court under Marshall and Taney grappled with the problems of the American people in the first sixty-four years of the nineteenth century.

But we think the sound construction of the Constitution must allow to the national legislature that discretion, with respect to the means by which the powers it confers are to be carried into execution, which will enable that body to perform the high duties assigned to it, in the manner most beneficial to the people.

JOHN MARSHALL (1819)

TWO

John Marshall and the Consolidation of National Power

From Independence to the Treaty of Ghent in 1815, the overriding question in American history was whether the nation—besieged without by hostile governments and within by provincialism and factionalism—had sufficient power to survive. After Ghent, the question was whether it had enough power to achieve greatness. Though the Supreme Court under John

Marshall (1801–1835) was as much concerned with this crucial issue as Congress and the executive, it did not seem likely in 1801 that it could profoundly affect the outcome. Little had happened during the Court's first twelve years to contradict Hamilton's observation of 1788 "that the judiciary is beyond comparison the weakest of the three departments of power" or to dispose of Chief Justice Jay's fear that the Court's weakness was permanent. President Adams' appointment of John Marshall—supported unenthusiastically even by the Federalists—did not particularly brighten the outlook.

Yet (as this chapter will show), within ten years the Court consolidated far-reaching judicial power and in fifteen more put the authority of Congress on a broad and permanent constitutional footing. Not only did the Court legitimize national power but also influenced (and this will be discussed in Chapter III) the manner in which power was used to achieve policy goals.

The gulf between promise and accomplishment presents the first interpretive problem about the Marshall Court. And, as it usually does, contemporary discussion has established the framework for scholarly debate. The Jeffersonians were certain of two things: that the Constitution was a limiting document and that John Marshall was a malignant force. They charged the Chief Justice with usurping power not in the Constitution and with converting his weak-willed colleagues to his plans for aggrandizement. The Federalists, on the other hand, expected the Court to consolidate national power and contain the emerging forces of democracy. And the more the Jeffersonians inveighed against Marshall, the more heroic he became to the party of conservative nationalism. The result—and it has been incorporated into historiography—was that the Chief Justice appeared to be the whole Court and to make history single-handedly.

It must be conceded that John Marshall was a natural for the heroic role. Few Americans, with the possible exception of Washington, were so appealing. He was an aristocrat by birth and political philosophy (in an age when gentlemen still ruled) but a democrat in manner (when democracy was the coming thing). Whether outracing his comrades in rare moments of leisure at Valley Forge, playing quoits with Richmond cronies, tempting Justice Joseph Story away from his Puritan habits with a bit of Madeira, or guiding the Court in conference, his democratic demeanor, openness, humor, and natural grace won the affection of many men. His writing was lucid and sometimes eloquent, informed by a mind that was superbly logical and incisive. And, again as the age demanded, Marshall tempered reason with experience. He had long been involved in the business of law, as well as in service to state and nation—as an officer in the Revolution, as a member of the Virginia House of Burgesses and delegate to the state ratifying convention, as special ambassador to France in 1797, as a Congressman, and, briefly, as Secretary of State under John Adams. His devotion to the Republic was beyond question. As the *North American Review* (January, 1836) aptly put it, "one could hardly help thinking that the office was made for the man, or the man for the office."

To complete the legend the only ingredient wanting was evidence that Marshall fought on the winning side of history. The Civil War and economic nationalism in the late nineteenth century took care of that. Historians had only to document the myth; aided by their Whiggish preferences, they found it easy to do. The process of glorification was launched with Allan Magruder's worshipful biography in 1890; it gained momentum with the Marshall Day celebration of 1901 (the outcome of which was a three-volume collection of encomiums compiled by John F. Dillon); and it culminated with Albert Beveridge's *The Life of John Marshall* (4 vols., 1916–1919) and Charles Warren's *The Supreme Court in United States History* (2 vols., 1922). With prodigious documentation Beveridge unabashedly celebrated the victory of light (conservative nationalism) over darkness (Jeffersonian states' rights agrarianism). And, by sheer force of emphasis and pervasive romanticism, his work raised Marshall above the Court, depicting him as the epic hero of American nationalism. Warren's history (still one of the outstanding works on the Court) was more scholarly, more balanced, and more generous in spreading the glory to include Marshall's colleagues but showed the same preference for conservative nationalism. A more serious shortcoming was Warren's failure to analyze and explain the greatness he described. He was, to be sure, less romantic and simplistic than Beveridge, but he took at face value the Court's assurance that it had no choice but to do what it did. As a result, the impression one gets from Warren is that under Marshall constitutional law was the inevitable, almost teleological, unfolding of axiomatic legal principles.

Revisionist historiography, for the most part, has not gainsaid the genius of the Chief Justice or the lasting achievements of his Court. However, it has been more concerned with Marshall as a man among men, a judge among judges, than with his heroism. Also, recent scholarship has been dissatisfied with the formal approach to law which removed the Court and justices from the political process, which denied judicial discretion and obscured genuine historical alternatives. Quite simply, the burden assumed by modern students is that of putting the Marshall Court back into history, of measuring its accomplishments in light of its institutional limitations and against the potential of the historical moment. Such was the implication of Oliver Wendell Holmes' heretical pronouncement that Marshall presented "a strategic point in the campaign of history, and part of his greatness consists in his being *there*." Such was the message of the classic essays on the Marshall Court by Max Lerner ("John Marshall and the Campaign of History," March, 1939) and by Felix Frankfurter ("John Marshall and the Judicial Function," December, 1955).

The historical restoration of the Marshall Court is taking place on various levels. Close study of the opinions themselves (as for example in Edward Corwin's pioneering essay, "Marbury v. Madison and the Doctrine of Judicial Review," February, 1914), their internal logic, rhetoric, and technical structure, continues to yield new insights. The microscopic approach has uncovered previously unnoticed political and economic premises as well as nuances and uncertainties of doctrine that belie the notion of a Marshall-dominated Court handing down pure law. Judicial biography is also contributing to a more sophisticated view of the Court by showing the variety of experience and complexity of motive behind decision making and the subtle shading which exists between the judge's bias and his commitment to the search for objective legal principles. The biographical approach is also calling attention to the collective nature of the Marshall Court. Studies like Donald Morgan's *Justice William Johnson* (1954) or the spate of articles on Justice Joseph Story show that Marshall shared authority with some very able colleagues who left their own imprint on the Court's work. The conclusion, which William Crosskey, Gerald Garvey, Donald Morgan, and Donald Roper arrive at separately, is that the law of the Marshall Court was much more the product of compromise and accomodation than was once thought.

Perhaps the most exciting trend in the scholarship of the Marshall period—and of the Taney period too—is the effort to see law as a dimension of culture. Some studies (Perry Miller's chapters on the legal mind in his *Life of the Mind in America from the Revolution to the Civil War,* 1965, are perhaps the best effort to date) have focused on the mutual relationship of law and intellectual history. Others have concentrated on the connection between law and economic development (the theme of Chapter III). Only recently (Willard Hurst has shown the way in *Law and the Social Process in United States History,* 1960, and in *Law and the Conditions of Freedom in the Nineteenth-Century United States,* 1956) have scholars attempted a synthetic analysis of the whole process of law in relation to historical change. The sociological approach, of course, does not relieve the student of the need to study the law itself and the Court as a legal institution. But it has shown that a full understanding of American law and legal institutions must be sought in their symbiotic relationship with the rest of American history.

THE STRUGGLE FOR JUDICIAL POWER: *MARBURY V. MADISON*

The "campaign of history," to follow Holmes' interpretive lead, in which Marshall and his colleagues were engaged concerned the issue of national union—and they found abundant opportunity for creative action. It is clear in retrospect that ingredients for success were not lacking. National statesmen could count on the deep patriotism of one generation of Americans who had waged a successful national revolution and of a second whose zeal was replenished by another war with the same enemy. Moreover, the nationalist impulse had been institutionalized by the Federal Constitution: rooted in practical wisdom, buttressed with untapped national power, and equipped with a method of change, the Constitution was an immeasurable boon to national survival. Constitutional government was also bolstered by an inherited tradition of popular respect for legal order which had survived the upheaval of revolution. Both the moral authority of Washington and a dozen successful years of nationhood gave momentum to the young republic. And the security provided by three thousand miles of ocean plus the prospect of prosperity rooted in an enterprising people and a rich continent were additional advantages that few emerging nations had.

Yet national union was as much potential as it was fact. Each advantage had a less auspicious side. If the Revolution was, as some historians insist, constructively conservative, it also set in motion social and political forces that could undercut the very foundations of the Constitution. Provincialism— and with it an indifference to national welfare and suspicion of national power—continued to embarrass effective central government. Given the diverse natures of the sections, the individual pursuit of economic happiness could easily divide the nation. And continental expansion could diffuse as well as enhance national unity.

In these ambivalent circumstances, it was far from certain whether the nation could last. Conceivably it might do so on terms other than those laid down by the Philadelphia Convention. More likely though, if national union was not attained with the Constitution of 1787, it would not be attained at all. The future of the republic, then, rested on the capability of that document to contain and accommodate the forces of political, economic, and intellectual change and harness them to the national purpose. A crucial question, therefore—and a great unknown in 1801—was how and by whom the Constitution would be interpreted.

When he assumed the duties of Chief Justice in March, 1801, two things were clear to John Marshall: first, that his Court must reinforce the movement toward a stronger national government; second, that it would have to establish its position as an authoritative interpreter of the Constitution in order to do so. It was the latter contingency that was problematical.

The institutional future of the Marshall Court was not entirely without promise. The constitutional grant of power, however ambiguous, was still considerable, and the pre-Marshall Court had begun to build on it. The jurisdictional and organizational gaps had been filled in with the passage of the Judiciary Act of 1789. The Court had established internal rules and procedures and set up working relationships with Congress and the executive, with the lower federal courts and the state judiciaries. The judiciary also began to consolidate its position as a separate and independent branch of the government. Congress challenged the Court's position in 1792 by enacting a law requiring the justices on circuit to pass on the validity of certain pensioners' claims. The justices objected strenuously on the grounds that such duties were not "properly judicial." And on the Pennsylvania Circuit, Justices James Wilson and John Blair boldly refused to obey the act and informed President Washington that it was unconstitutional. A year later the Court struck another blow for judicial independence, this time against executive encroachment, when it refused to render certain advisory opinions requested by the President. Most important, the Court established precedents for judicial review. In several cases on circuit the justices voided state legislative acts because they conflicted with the Constitution. And in

Hylton v. *United States* (1796) the Court considered the constitutionality of a federal tax on carriages, and, although it upheld the act, it clearly implied that it had the power to declare acts of Congress unconstitutional.

The early Court did not neglect to make policy as it decided cases. And its policy preferences were clearly those of the Federalist party, which is to say it favored property rights and national over state power. The Court maintained national supremacy by voiding state acts in conflict with the Constitution and federal treaties. State power was humbled in *Chisholm* v. *Georgia* (1793), when the Court brought a sovereign state before its bar and held it answerable to suits brought by private citizens. And when state acts violating property rights were invalidated by federal courts, the sanctity of property was assured and nationalism bolstered. With its interpretation of international law and neutral rights, and with its recognition of a federal criminal common law (that is, a body of federal crimes not specified by statute), the Court added further to national authority. These policies and the axioms of interpretation used to justify them—the contract clause, the doctrine of natural law limitations on legislative power, and the notion of the Court as the constitutional voice of the sovereign people—were all part of the historical legacy which was passed down to the Marshall Court.

Yet in 1801, the Court had not established itself as *the* authoritative interpreter of the Constitution. The Republicans supported the right of the states to interpret the constitutional powers of the federal government in the Virginia and Kentucky Resolutions of 1798 and 1799. And the Republican view was supported by the electoral victory of 1800. Presidents, senators and representatives, as well as justices, took an oath to uphold the Constitution, and they all insisted on their right to interpret the document. The claim of Congress was especially strong. The tradition of legislative dominance, dating from the revolutionary and confederation period, was still vital in the 1790's. As Donald Morgan makes clear in *Congress and the Constitution* (1966), Congress had resolved more crucial constitutional problems during the first twelve years of American government than had the Supreme Court: action on the first eleven amendments took place mainly in Congress and the Eleventh Amendment specifically revised a constitutional decision of the Court. Organic laws involving basic constitutional questions, including those which organized the judicial branch, were left to Congress. So were special constitutional issues like the President's removal power and questions about the First Amendment raised by the Alien and Sedition Acts (the constitutionality of which the Court deliberately refused to consider). With the Republicans in control of Congress after 1801 and the Federalists barricaded in the judicial branch, congressional claims were certain to be pressed with new vigor.

Not only had the Court failed to capture the high ground, but the power it did hold was in jeopardy. Its *Chisholm* decision had been reversed by the Eleventh Amendment. The Court's willingness to hear criminal cases brought under the common law (in the absence of federal statutes defining crimes against the nation) was bitterly assailed, and the Court surrendered the power in *United States* v. *Hudson* (1812). But more threatening than the challenge to the Court's law was the decline in its modest prestige. Want of litigation was one reason: the Court had been open for business for a year and a half before deciding a case. By 1801 it had decided only sixty-three cases, averaging less than one of real significance each year. As the rapid turnover in membership and the difficulty in finding talented replacements indicated, aspiring statesmen were not interested in positions on the Court. Twelve men had served there prior to 1801. Five, including two Chief Justices, had resigned, and five others, including John Marshall, had declined appointments. By 1800, the reservoir of talent was dangerously low. The men with the best minds—John Jay, James Wilson, James Iredell, Oliver Ellsworth—were gone. Of those remaining, Bushrod Washington and William Paterson were able but did not possess the necessary leadership; Samuel Chase's genuine ability was negated by political intemperance; William Cushing, who was only modestly able when well, was constantly sick; and Alfred Moore was neither interested in nor equipped for the job.

On top of its other woes, the Court was deeply involved in the bitter political battles of the day—and on the losing side. The Republicans, who had gained the Presidency and both houses of Congress in the election of 1800, were in a position to humble the Court. By their own lights they had ample justification for doing so. The Court's penchant for conservative nationalism corresponded closely with Federalist policy—a fact which Republicans not unreasonably attributed to the solid Federalist composition of the bench. Both Jay and Ellsworth had served as special foreign emissaries for the Federalist Party during their tenures as Chief Justice; the Republicans interpreted this as another mark of judicial partisanship. The enthusiasm with which Federalist judges enforced the Sedition Act of 1798 against Republican critics aroused bitter resentment, and their refusal to consider the Act's constitutionality further inflamed sentiment against the Court. The anti-Jeffersonian political harangues which Justice Chase delivered from the bench brought these feelings to a boil. Finally, the Judiciary Act of 1801—which created sixteen new judgeships for Federalists and reduced the Court from six to five so that President Jefferson would not be able to appoint a Republican justice—made it inevitable that the Court would be attacked by both the President and Congress.

Here then was the unpromising historical material from which judicial power had to be molded. What could be done? Immediate action was imperative lest judicial weakness become an institutional habit. But the Court had few offensive weapons in its arsenal. Its vulnerability to the aroused Republican forces, moreover, made dramatic action inadvisable. Marshall escaped this dilemma by undertaking, as the first order of business, to unify the Court and order its internal affairs. He thus turned the weakness of his colleagues to advantage and precluded reprisal from the Republicans. Relying on the unifying effect of Republican threats, the Federalist sympathies of the other justices, and on his own charisma, Marshall persuaded his associates to abandon seriatim opinions for a single majority opinion. And, to make the most of this new procedure, Marshall was to write the final opinion of the Court himself. From 1801 to 1805, he wrote twenty-four of the Court's twenty-six opinions; the other two were cases on which he did not sit because they had come up from his own circuit. During this period there were no dissents and only one separate opinion. Up to 1810, Marshall had written 147 of 171 opinions, including all the important ones. The appointment of stronger minds to the Court was soon to reduce Marshall's dominance. But for the time it was an expedient and successful means of regaining lost ground against heavy odds.

But unity alone was not enough. What the Court needed was a victory—and this did not seem likely. During Marshall's first two years, the Court had decided only seven cases and there had not been a significant one since 1798. Moreover, the Republican juggernaut had begun to roll. In 1802, in the midst of ominous anti-Court rhetoric, the Judiciary Act of 1801 was repealed, returning the judiciary to the system of 1789. On the heels of the repeal came another bill establishing new terms for the Court—in effect adjourning it for fourteen months (from December, 1801, to February, 1803). During this time, the Republicans sharpened their impeachment weapons and talked of wholesale slaughter.

There was the possibility, of course, that the Court might take the offensive itself and invalidate the Judicial Repeal Act of 1802. Ultra-Federalists imprudently urged it to do so. But, fortunately for the Court, John Marshall was more intrigued with the unemployment problem of one William Marbury. Back in February, 1801, the Federalists had passed a bill authorizing the President to create as many justices of the peace for the District of Columbia as he thought expedient. Forty-two offices were created and, at the last minute, filled with trustworthy Federalists. When Secretary of State Madison assumed his new duties on March 5, he found the commissions duly signed, sealed, and ready for delivery. None were delivered. Jefferson later commissioned thirty justices of the peace, including twenty-three of those nominated by Adams. During the December, 1801 term, Marbury and three other dispossessed officials requested a writ of mandamus from the

Court ordering Madison to show cause why he should not be compelled to deliver their commissions.

Marbury v. *Madison* (1803) clearly was not one of those cases that was ready made for greatness. If it promised anything, it was disaster, for the facts seemed to be leading the Court to a fateful confrontation with Republican power. Should the Court issue the writ and the President ignore it, judicial power would be humbled. If the Court refused to issue the writ, the Republicans—and the executive department, for it was also a struggle between departments—would win by default.

Marshall's opinion in behalf of the unanimous Court was austere in its simplicity. The key questions and the Court's answers amounted to one paragraph: Had Marbury a right to his commission? If so, did the law afford him a remedy? If it did, was the remedy a mandamus issued by the Court? Affirmative replies to the first two questions led the Court to a direct confrontation with Republican power. A negative reply to the third, justified by Marshall's unique reasoning, allowed it to escape and turned retreat into victory. The Court cannot issue a writ of mandamus, declared the Chief Justice, because the power to do so (granted in Section 13 of the Judiciary Act of 1789) was not specified in Article III of the Constitution as being within the original jurisdiction of the Court. Though Congress might control the appellate jurisdiction of the Supreme Court by Article III, it had no authority to regulate the Court's original jurisdiction. There was no choice, therefore, but to hold that Section 13 was an unconstitutional exercise of congressional power. William Marbury had lost his job, and the Supreme Court had made good its claim to review acts of Congress.

Behind the facade of simplicity (Corwin's previously cited essay, "Marbury v. Madison and the Doctrine of Judicial Review," leaves no doubt on the matter) were some crafty legal tactics which must have given Jefferson cause to wonder whether the bench really was a good place to bury his old enemy. Marshall's first coup was to reverse the regular order of questions (he warned counsel that there would be "some departure in form" from the points stated in argument). He could have disposed of the case straight off—and without ruling on Section 13—by holding that Marbury could not bring a case on original jurisdiction before the Court since he was not an ambassador, public minister, or consul. Instead, Marshall asked questions one and two, which gave him an opportunity to expound the doctrine of vested rights and to remind the President of the United States that he was not above the laws of the country (a lecture he would surely not have dared give to Washington or Adams).

More daring yet was his declaration that Section 13 was unconstitutional. For this large proposition, Marshall did not offer a single precedent; nor did he reason from the wording or intention of the act itself. He merely asserted. In doing so, he ignored previous circuit and Supreme Court rulings upholding Section 13, as well as the axiom of constitutional interpretation expounded by the Framers and repeated by state judges and Supreme Court justices, that no act ought to be voided if a plausible argument for its constitutionality could be made. A less ingenious mind than Marshall's could have supplied an argument for issuing a writ of mandamus in Section 13 by viewing it as a power incident to the original jurisdiction granted by Article III rather than as an addition to it—a position which, in fact, he later acknowledged.

After disposing summarily with Section 13, Marshall expanded in Olympian fashion on the general theory of judicial review. The substance of his argument came, without acknowledgment, from Hamilton's *Federalist* No. 78. The principles he deduced were simple and "long and well established": The "original and supreme will" of the sovereign people created the written Constitution, which is the supreme and paramount law of the land. That Constitution imposed on the Court the burden of explaining what that law was. All else followed. (Jefferson once cautioned against granting Marshall the toehold of a premise.) If the legislature passed an act in conflict with the supreme law of the Constitution, the Court, in explicating the law, had no choice but to uphold the Constitution and void the act of Congress. The duty was simple and straightforward; not to perform it would be "immoral." In the midst of such simple truths, the central question of whether Section 13 was in conflict with the Constitution was forgotten.

Despite its boldness, Marshall's opinion left the Court well protected from Republican reprisal. It avoided the inevitable insult that would have come with an issuance of the writ and, in the process, salvaged the principles of judicial review. Marshall made this powerful blow for judicial power seem almost innocuous. Section 13 was of small overall importance and concerned the Court's own business; voiding it appeared to be an act of judicial self-denial—especially when six days later *Stuart* v. *Laird* sustained the constitutionality of the Republican Repeal Act of 1802. Marshall's emphasis on the doctrine of limited government, moreover, reminded the Jeffersonian opposition that judicial review was congenial with their own philosophy of government. In fact, the brunt of the Republican attack was not against the principle of judicial review but against Marshall's brusque censure of the President.

Because the mandamus decision has been the focal point of debate over the Court's rise to power, historical evaluations of it have varied sharply. The present tendency is to abandon the hero-villain approach for a less dramatic and more sophisticated assessment. Few scholars now blame Marshall for radical usurpation or credit him with the single-handed creation of judicial power. The Constitution, after all, paved the way for judicial review, while Hamilton's *Federalist* No. 78, judicial precedents, and the debates over the Repeal Act of 1802 all supported Marshall in his decision. Moreover, it is clear now that the decision was neither comprehensive—since it dealt only with an act concerning the judiciary, which even Jefferson agreed was within the Court's purview—nor conclusive—since no precedent can underwrite a power persistently abused. Nor was the precedent of immediate use. Not until *Dred Scott* v. *Sanford* fifty-four years later did the Court void another congressional statute. And not until the rise of substantive due process in the late nineteenth century was the full power of judicial review realized. Finally, as Justice

Holmes reminds us, the foundation of constitutional nationalism was the Court's power to review *state*, not national, legislation. By 1803, that power had been solidly established by the Supreme Court on circuit.

Marshall's mandamus decision may not have changed the course of constitutional history, as the romantics insisted, but it was a constructive "coup" (both Beveridge and Corwin use the word) that determined which direction the historical current would run. For the first time, the Supreme Court claimed the power to review acts of Congress and, because of Marshall's strategy, made good its claims. Though not immediately of value, the prescriptive authority of this decision, adorned as it was with Marshall's eloquence, was ready ammunition for the Court in its constant struggle to justify its use of power. Saying "no" to Congress in 1803, moreover, gave authority to the Court when it said "yes"—which it subsequently did no less than fourteen times. Certainly, the successful assertion of judicial prerogative in 1803 was just what the Court needed to boost its sagging spirits and prestige until better days.

To talk of consequences, however, is to run ahead of events. Because of the impending impeachment campaign, it was uncertain in 1803, and for two years thereafter, whether the mandamus opinion was a victory or a swan song. Republicans had threatened removals since the late 1790's, and now they meant to act. Federal District Judge John Pickering, who unwisely mixed alcohol with his Federalism, was the first to go. In 1805, Justice Samuel Chase was charged with misconduct in the sedition trial of James Callender, in the treason trial of John Fries, and for his political harangues to grand juries in Delaware and Baltimore. A conviction would seriously jeopardize judicial separateness and equality, for, as John Quincy Adams noted, the whole Court, "from the first establishment of the national Judiciary," was on trial. Chase's acquittal (helped by a brilliant defense and inept Republican management) rested finally on the recognition that he was guilty not of "treason, bribery, or other high crimes and misdemeanors," which were the constitutional grounds for removal, but of political intemperance. The Senate's decision was scarcely less significant than the Court's mandamus opinion, since it virtually eliminated impeachment (" a mere scarecrow of a thing," concluded Jefferson in disgust) as a means of controlling the Court. The judicial claim to power—suggested by Hamilton, aspired to by the early Court, and asserted by Marshall in *Marbury* v. *Madison*—was validated. The Republicans, it should be added, salvaged a small victory by teaching the judges to subdue their political passions and improve their judicial manners.

However, Chase's good luck did not entirely lift the Republican siege. Two years later, in the treason trial of Aaron Burr, the Jeffersonians and the judiciary (or rather President Jefferson and Chief Justice Marshall) were again in battle. Burr's refusal in 1800 to withdraw from the Presidential contest in the House of Representatives, and his subsequent flirtation with Federalist states' rights intrigues in New York, had turned Jefferson bitterly against him. And the President had no doubt that Burr's mysterious expedition down the Mississippi River was for the treasonable purpose of separating the Southwest from the Union. Indeed, as Beveridge gleefully recounts in his biography of Marshall, Jefferson said so publicly and, during the trial, personally marshalled witnesses and evidence to assure a conviction. (He even asked Congress for authorization to suspend the right of the writ of habeas corpus.) Marshall, on the other hand, while technically scrupulous in the conduct of the trial, could not disguise his contempt for the President. Over the strenuous protest of government counsel, he released Burr on bail and, during the pre-trial hearings, appeared at a dinner given in honor of the defendant by his chief counsel. He allowed (some said encouraged) statements by counsel derogatory to the President. (Eyewitness Nathaniel Saltonstall reported that Burr's lawyer Luther Martin "don't stick very closely to the question before the Court but likes better to *rub* the Executive.") And most audaciously, though without success, Marshall subpoenaed the President to appear before the circuit court.

Though almost obscured by political overtones and by the human drama, the crucial aspect of Burr's trial was its effect on the American law of treason—and on determining whether the judiciary or the executive would decide what that law was. Article III, Section 3, of the Constitution defined treason as "levying war" against the United States or "adhering to their enemies, giving them aid and comfort," and required either "confession in open court" or "the testimony of two witnesses to the same overt act" as grounds for conviction. The prosecution's charge that Burr's procurement of men at Blennerhassett's Island was treason raised two fundamental and related questions: (1) What was the meaning of "levying war"? (2) Were all parties involved in treason principals, as the common law had it? (Since Burr had not been present at the assemblage of men, this was an important point.) Marshall read the Constitution strictly on both questions. Levying war meant an overt act of creating war and "must be proved by an open deed." And, procuring or advising treason was not itself treason, for the Constitution did not recognize the common law doctrine of constructive treason. In any case, procurement would have to be proved by two witnesses to the overt act. Both holdings assured Burr's acquittal since no levy of war had been proved and since no witnesses to the overt act of procurement could be produced. That the Chief Justice was as pleased with the political implications of his decision as Jefferson was dismayed can hardly be doubted. That he twisted the law for political ends, as the Republicans and some historians have charged, however, does not follow (and Robert K. Faulkner demonstrates this in "John Marshall and the Burr Trial," September, 1966). They miss the crucial point: Marshall's strict reading of the Constitution and firm position on evidence put the American law of treason beyond the easy grasp of political expediency, as the Framers of the Constitution had intended.

The clash between the President and the Chief Justice could not obscure the fact that the Court and the Republicans had come to share enough ground for a rapprochement. There had, in fact, always been a theoretical affinity between judicial power and the Republican policy of limited government. And the Republicans' acceptance of judicial review in 1803 suggests they recognized this. Even Marshall's opinion in the Burr trial was in the spirit of Jeffersonianism—a strike for individual liberties against governmental tyranny. The shift in the positions of the two parties after 1800 paved the way for reconciliation. Having lost power in Washington, the Federalists turned from nationalism to states' rights. On the other hand, the Jeffersonian Republicans, faced with the responsibilities of governing and challenged by the militant provincialism of the Federalists, became the party of nationalism. Their radically nationalist policy from the Embargo of 1807 to the War of 1812 brought open resistance from New England Federalists. It became painfully clear to the Republicans that national authority depended heavily on the federal courts. In 1809, with three Republicans on the bench—William Johnson (1804), Henry Brockholst Livingston (1806), and Thomas Todd (1807)—and Jefferson in retirement, the stage was set for a new period of harmony.

United States v. *Peters* (1809) signaled the change. Since 1779, the state of Pennsylvania had resisted a decree of the Committee on Appeals of the Continental Congress reversing a prize decision of the state admiralty court. When in 1803 Federal District Judge Richard Peters affirmed the Committee's decision, the state legislature ignored the decision and reasserted Pennsylvania's rights threateningly. By 1808, when the Supreme Court was asked for a writ of mandamus compelling Peters to execute his decision, the cause had assumed ominous implications for the nation. The successful assertion by a state legislature of its right to interpret federal law would encourage New England in her overt opposition to the Embargo and would, as Hall's *Law Journal* put it, send the Constitution "to the trunkmaker as a Damn'd Paper, Black as the ink that's on it: senseless bauble!"

Marshall quashed both possibilities in a powerful opinion upholding the power of the nation to enforce its laws by the "instrumentality of its own tribunals." When the Pennsylvania legislature petitioned President Madison for redress, he firmly refused; when Governor Snyder threatened to call out the militia, Madison made it clear that such a move would be met by national authority. The victory, based on the harmony of the Court and the executive, signified the successful consolidation of judicial power.

United States v. *Peters,* in 1809, marked the start of a new age for the Court. But it was not until *Martin* v. *Hunter's Lessee* seven years later that the Court formally completed the circle of judicial power. The *Martin* case came before the Court on the nationalist wave that started with the British attack on the *Chesapeake* in 1807. But it originated during the American Revolution when Virginia passed an act confiscating Tory lands within the state and subsequently sold those lands to private citizens. Other citizens claimed the same lands by titles that ran back to the original Tory owners and for thirty-odd years they contested the validity of the state confiscation act. The Supreme Court voided that act in *Fairfax's Devisee* v. *Hunter's Lessee* (1813), on the ground that it conflicted with the Treaty of 1794 with England. After consulting with Jefferson and Monroe, the Virginia Court of Appeals not only refused to obey the Court's decision, but also denied the constitutionality of Section 25 of the Judiciary Act under which the case had been heard. It was this refusal and denial which came, on another writ of error, before the Supreme Court in the *Martin* case.

In a unanimous opinion, Republican appointee Joseph Story chastised the Republican state of Virginia for following the states' rights course of Federalist Massachusetts, his own native state. Fusing together law, logic, and policy, he made a case for appellate jurisdiction that was "unanswerable and conclusive," as Chancellor James Kent later put it. Because some constitutional questions (which came under the Supreme Court's jurisdiction by Article III) could be heard in state courts, Story argued, it was imperative that those state court decisions be reviewable by the Supreme Court. Section 25 provided for this essential process of review; to deny that section would curtail the powers granted to the Court by the Constitution. It is a "doubtful course," Story continued, to argue that the Supreme Court should not have the final power of review because that power might be abused. "From the very nature of things, the absolute right of decision, in the last resort, must rest somewhere. . . ." Before and after this powerful assertion, Story delivered obiter dicta which carried judicial nationalism even further. Operating on the now familiar premise that it was not the states but the whole people who created the Constitution, Story arrived at the threshold of implied powers—that doctrine which was to be the constitutional hallmark of the "golden age." And before he was finished, he set a new precedent for judicial aggressiveness by informing Congress that it was constitutionally obliged to maintain the final review power of the Court. ("What would be thought of a judgment of the Court of King's-Bench," declared the shocked *United States Magazine and Democratic Review* twenty-two years later, "that should lecture Parliament on what it *must* enact!" Ten years earlier the *Martin* ruling would have run headlong into the unyielding resistance of the executive, Congress, and the states. But, instead, in the euphoric climate of nationalism after the war of 1812, it became, as Charles Warren observed, the "keystone of the whole arch of Federal judicial power."

John Jay, who was still alive, must have gladly retracted his gloomy pronouncement of 1801, that the Court lacked and would never acquire "energy, weight, and dignity." For in these formative years it was the Court—and not Congress or the President or the states—that presented itself as the most authoritative interpreter of the Constitution. The record was impressive. Over bitter opposition, the Court had confirmed its power to review state acts and to pass final judgment on federal questions coming from state courts. It had turned the implications in the Constitution concerning judicial review of congressional acts into solid precedent. And in the process of acquiring power, the Court developed techniques for using it: the united bench delivering a single opinion, the convenient device of obiter dicta, the leeway afforded by constitutional and statutory interpretation, and the educative possibilities of judicial opinion were all explored. Finally, the Court had begun to justify itself to American democracy. The Court insisted that when it spoke, it did so in the people's name and from an allegedly certain Constitution that left no room for judicial partiality.

The Court's claim of being the repository of constitutional truth looked stronger when compared to the difficulties the states and other branches of the national government had in interpreting the Constitution. State efforts (those of Virginia and Kentucky in 1798 and 1799 and those of Pennsylvania in 1809) faltered because of their anarchic implications and their lack of support from other states. Presidential limitations in the area of constitutional interpretation were apparent in the purchase of the Louisiana Territory in 1803. Here, Jefferson was forced to set aside his theory of limited government to do what expediency required. A constitutional system that could not embrace the responsibilities of governing and that had to be suspended at the dictates of expediency was no system at all. The long-range advantages of judicial over executive interpretation were further apparent in the Burr treason trial. Congress, moreover, failed to provide a forum for rational and conclusive constitutional debate. Indeed, while the Court was bringing order in its own house, the national legislature was falling into anarchy. When unity was finally restored in the 1820's, with the reestablishment of the two party system, it was a unity based on constituent politics which functioned by cajolement and compromise. The imperative of congressional parties, it turned out, was not to resolve constitutional issues but to obscure them.

Neither the states, nor the President, nor the Congress surrendered its right to interpret the Constitution and all continued to influence constitutional law. But it was the Supreme Court that emerged from the struggles of the early nineteenth century as best qualified to speak fully and authoritatively on the Constitution. Authority—and this is where John Marshall made his mark—followed demonstrated ability.

The foundation of judicial government had been laid, and, history permitting, the Court was ready to build on it.

THE COURT AND THE CONSOLIDATION OF NATIONAL POWER

The War of 1812—fought for ends which had been largely achieved by diplomacy, concluded by a treaty that settled nothing that was unsettled, and devoid of military glory except for a battle won after the war ended—hardly seemed the occasion for a resurgence of nationalism. Yet the war dissolved the miasma of apprehension which had hung over the Republic since independence. In 1815, for the first time in our national history, we were simultaneously at peace with Europe and with ourselves. France, beaten and weak, was no threat; Britain, also exhausted, was already calculating the advantages of free trade, a policy that would bind her to the United States in mutual self-interest. Separatist tendencies—the monopoly of no one section or party—and partisan feelings seemed to disappear as the fortunes of the Federalists ebbed. The diverse economic energies of the agrarian South, the commercial-industrial North, and the burgeoning West appeared to be the foundation blocks of a self-sustaining national economy, rather than forces of disunity. With the ardor of the Revolution restored, with confidence in the well-wishes of a "superintending providence," and casting a disdainful glance back at evil Europe, the young nation set out for the Pacific, certain of finding Utopia on the way.

As contemporary statesmen well knew, the need was to build an enduring and powerful union by capturing this historic moment. There is no country, said Madison in his Annual Message of 1815, "where nature invites more the art of man to complete her own work for his accommodation and benefit." "Art" took the form of a national bank, a protective tariff, and federally sponsored internal improvements. National mercantilism would bind together diverse sections in mutual advantage and insure that national unity would accompany continental expansion. The question was whether the Constitution, incorporating eighteenth-century notions of limited government, could be made to yield sufficient power to accommodate nineteenth-century aspirations. And, at the same time, could those political and economic groups which attached themselves to limited government be assured that constitutional union was advantageous?

The Court had not yet faced the challenge. No determination of the constitutional grants of power to Congress had been made. What the Court had said in its important prewar decisions had, in fact, emphasized the doctrine of constitutional limitations. Yet given the human factor in decision-making, there was good reason to believe that the judges would make the Constitution serve nationalism. After all, justices of the Supreme Court belonged to the national establishment, and, if institutional self-interest did not incline them to favor nationalism, it at least freed them from selfish prejudice against it. Many of them had absorbed nationalism during the Revolution—Marshall more than the rest. All, Federalists and Republicans alike, had seen national greatness go unrealized for want of unity and power. Both experience and position made them aware of the potential of creative nationalism in the postwar period. It soon became clear that the Court was going to make the Constitution support the "great national interests," to use Justice Story's words, "which shall bind us in an indissoluble chain."

McCulloch v. *Maryland* (1819) was an ideal place for the Court to begin. The case focused on the Second Bank of the United States and, through it, touched on the great political and economic issues of the day. Chartered by Congress in 1816, the Bank was part of the American mercantilist system; its job was to aid the government in fiscal operations and provide a national system of credit and a uniform national currency. But instead of restraining state banks (supposedly one of its duties), the Bank, under its first president, competed against them in speculation and the reckless extension of credit. In 1818, the Bank saved itself from the impending crash by calling in its loans but, in doing so, brought down a number of over-extended state banks, especially in the South and West. On the assumption that the Bank caused the panic (and because of pressure from jealous state banks), seven states passed laws restraining the Bank's operations. In Maryland the retaliation took the form of a tax on the notes of all banks—including the Baltimore branch of the Bank of the United States—not chartered by the state. The Bank's appeal of the state court decision which upheld the Maryland tax brought two vital constitutional questions before the Supreme Court: Had Congress the power to charter a bank? If so, did Maryland have the right to tax its operations within the state? On the Court's answers rested not only the fate of the Bank but the whole system of national mercantilism. And more. For the first time, the Court had to determine the scope of congressional powers and their relation to the powers of the states. The responsibility was "awful," admitted Marshall—but it is hard to believe he really minded it.

Speaking for a unanimous Court, Marshall opened with the humble disclaimer that the Court was only doing what it had to do—fair warning that something important was in the offing. Then, quietly dropping his humility, he turned to Maryland's assertions of state sovereignty. He expounded (with the aid of William Pinkney's brilliant argument at the bar) the "great principle" of national supremacy on which his case— and the entire edifice of constitutional nationalism—would rest. "In America," Marshall conceded, "the powers of sovereignty are divided between the government of the Union, and those of the States. They are each sovereign, with respect to the objects committed to it, and neither sovereign with respect to the objects committed to the other." But national sovereignty is supreme over state sovereignty—however paradoxically, Marshall's argument comes to this. Though the national government is limited, within its sphere of powers it is supreme. When this national power conflicts with state power, the latter must give way. Thus, national supremacy becomes the informing spirit of the Constitution and the guiding principle of its interpretation. The government of the United States has this crucial prerogative because, and here Marshall sounded the democratic theme, "It is the government of all; its powers are delegated by all; it represents all, and acts for all."

So much for state sovereignty. The key question still remained: Was the incorporation of the Bank (a power not among the enumerated powers in Article I, Section 8) a constitutional act within the protective perimeter of national supremacy? Emphatically yes, said Marshall, and in support of his view he called on history, law, policy—and Alexander Hamilton. The constitutionality of incorporation had been debated exhaustively and affirmed in 1791 by Congress (in regard to the First Bank); by 1816, it was an accepted truth. Marshall admitted that prescription could not justify a usurpation of power, but he felt it proved there had been none. Regarding the absence of the right of incorporation among the enumerated powers, he argued: If every power necessary to a government had to be listed, the Constitution would become a legal code, the prolixity of which "could scarcely be embraced by the human mind." And in words Felix Frankfurter thought the most important ever uttered by an American judge, Marshall emphasized, "We must never forget that it is a constitution we are expounding."

What he meant became abundantly clear. The Constitution was intended to be a source of power sufficient to the "exigencies of the nation." "A government, instructed with such ample powers, on the due execution of which the happiness and prosperity of the nation so vitally depends, must be entrusted with ample means for their execution." The document itself supports this extension of congressional powers beyond those enumerated, Marshall added. Implied powers are nowhere forbidden. The word "expressly" was deliberately stricken from the Tenth Amendment by the Constitutional Convention, thus avoiding an explicit limitation on national powers. But above all, following the specific enumeration of powers in Article I, Section 8, the Constitution gave Congress the power to pass "all laws which shall be necessary and proper for carrying into execution the foregoing powers."

The scope of congressional power, then, came to hang on the meaning of "necessary." Maryland agreed with Thomas Jefferson that the word meant to exclude from Congress the choice of means and bound it strictly to the exercise of specified powers. Marshall took the Hamiltonian view that it was a grant of "additional power," one which left Congress discretion in the choice of means to execute "those great powers on which the welfare of the nation essentially depends." Common usage and constitutional syntax, he asserted, supported his position. But most conclusive was the fact that to hold otherwise would leave the Constitution a "splendid bawble." His argument left it instead—in his own famous words —a "constitution intended to endure for ages to come, and, consequently, to be adapted to the various crises of human affairs."

With a strong assist from Hamilton, Marshall pulled the various strands of his argument together, stating the constitutional rule for interpretation of congressional power: "Let the end be legitimate, let it be within the scope of the Constitution, and all means which are appropriate, which are plainly adapted to that end, which are not prohibited, but consist with the letter and spirit of the Constitution, are constitutional." By this rule the Bank—hardly mentioned before—was constitutional. The act of incorporation was not prohibited and was an obvious means for achieving the great ends of national government. Therefore, it was constitutional and "part of the supreme law of the land."

Turning to the question of Maryland's right to tax the Bank, Marshall set forth the interpretive touchstone for state power which complemented his doctrine of national supremacy. Together they comprised the formula for preventing a "clashing sovereignty." The Constitution had, Marshall conceded, "no express provision" for limiting the states' crucial power to tax. But, by piling inference on inference, he made up this deficiency. Start, he said, with the principle already expounded that the Constitution and laws made in pursuance of it are supreme. Admit that the creation of a Bank by implication is among those constitutional and supreme laws. Concede further that "a power to create implies a power to preserve" and, further still, that "the power to tax involves the power to destroy . . . and render useless the power to create." Acknowledge finally that "there is a plain repugnance, in conferring on one government a power to control the constitutional measures of another, which other, with respect to those very measures, is declared to be supreme over that which exerts the control," and you have the answer. Without bothering to consider whether the Maryland tax did in fact threaten the Bank with destruction (which it did not), Marshall found it unconstitutional.

Marshall then translated this specific instance into a general rule, harmonized it with his earlier principle, and arrived at a guideline defining the limits of state power: "States have no power, by taxation or otherwise, to retard, impede, burden, or in any manner control, the operations of the constitutional laws enacted by Congress to carry into execution the powers vested in the general government."

Marshall's opinion—or rather his state paper—was a bold exercise in judicial lawmaking. The government of limited and enumerated powers became, without benefit of amendment, the government of expansive powers. Marshall reconciled state and national sovereignty with the federal system by using both the idea of national supremacy and its corollary—that states are chronic aggressors against national authority—as his touchstones. But more significant than these broad principles was the spirit in which they were interpreted. Approaching the Constitution with the expectation that it must supply what the nation needs, Marshall set the dominant tone for American constitutional law in the future.

These principles were not mere legal generalities but practical responses to pressing questions of national policy. Nationalist arguments answered the states' rights theories put forth by the South during the opening phase of the Missouri Debates. Implied powers put the Bank of the United States on a constitutional footing and solved the problem of national unity created by the acquisition of vast new territory in the Adams-Onís Treaty of 1819. As Marshall observed in his opinion, the Republic now extended "from the St. Croix to the Gulf of Mexico, from the Atlantic to the Pacific." Federal internal improvements were required to bind the nation together, and Congress, armed with implied powers, was equipped to authorize them. If there was any doubt whether the Court meant that implied powers should embrace such improvements, it was removed by Justice Johnson's 1822 letter to President Monroe—the one, unexplained exception to the Court's rule against advisory opinions. While Congress acquired the power to enact a national economic plan, the states were restrained from interfering by Marshall's opinion on state taxing power.

The Chief Justice was rarely so categorical—and less profound—than when he spoke on the issue of state taxing power. By avoiding the difficult question of degree—whether and at what point Maryland's tax actually threatened the operations of the Bank—and by assuming that state taxation *per se* would destroy the Bank and further that a bank controlled by private capital was an arm of the federal government, Marshall in effect set up a category where the federal government was immune from state taxation. This simplistic doctrine of tax immunity (extended to include state immunity against federal taxation in *Weston* v. *Charleston,* 1829) did not do justice to the complexity of the problem. After resulting in much embarrassment, it was abandoned by the Court in the twentieth century.

As in *Marbury* v. *Madison,* the genius of the *McCulloch* opinion lay not in its originality but in its timing, practicability, clarity, and eloquence. Original it was not. The doctrine of implied powers had been stated fully and powerfully by Hamilton in his cabinet memorandum of 1791. Congress verified the doctrine by chartering both the first and the second Banks and by providing financial support for a system of internal improvements. The Court itself had intimated implied powers as early as *United States* v. *Fisher* (1805), and Story boldly expanded the principle in *Martin* v. *Hunter's Lessee* (1816). Disparagement of state power was another common nationalist theme, as a reading of the *Federalist* makes very clear. And the notion of a supreme Constitution based on popular sovereignty had been judicial stock-in-trade since the Jay-Ellsworth Courts. Even Marshall's famous encomium of the Constitution as adequate for all ages was an axiom of the day. Marshall did not create these nationalist principles. What he did do was seize them at the moment when they were most relevant to American needs and congenial to the American mind, and (aided by the rhetoric of Alexander Hamilton) he translated them gracefully and logically into the law of the Constitution. Basing his interpretation of the law on the needs and spirit of the age, Marshall gave it permanence. Hamilton himself was unable to do as much.

In 1819, however, the verdict of history was not yet in. Marshall's constitutional nationalism had not pleased the whole nation. Although the Northeast generally found the consolidating tendencies congenial to its economic aspirations and rallied behind *McCulloch* v. *Maryland,* the Southern states had their own version of the true Constitution, and it bore no resemblance to Marshall's. Three weeks before the *McCulloch* decision, a bitter, searching debate on slavery and the nature of the Union was set off by the Tallmadge amendment prohibiting slavery in the new state of Missouri. And even as Marshall was reading the Court's opinion, the first shock waves of the Panic of 1819 were felt. If the "era of good feelings" had ever existed, it was over now. The depression reminded Southerners of the special policy needs of slave-based agrarianism; they concluded that much more was exacted from them by the Bank, the tariff, and internal improvements than was given. In the Missouri Debates, the slaveholding states were faced with their minority position in the Union and with the fact that Marshall's legal nationalism put them at the mercy of an ever-increasing, and perhaps anti-slave, Northern majority.

Compelled by self-interest, the South rallied around the doctrines of strict and enumerated powers and constitutional change by constitutional amendment—which would give the South a protective veto against the majority. Virginia's Democracy led the way toward the new orthodoxy and against the "damnable heretical" usurpation of the Marshall Court. Judge Spencer Roane of the Virginia Court of Appeals, backed by Jefferson, began the assault with a series of articles against the *McCulloch* opinion in the powerful Richmond *Enquirer.* John Taylor of Caroline followed with a full refutation of the

Hamilton-Marshall stand in *Construction Construed and Constitution Vindicated* (1820). While the battle of words raged, Virginia's legislature met, condemned the Court, and instructed congressional delegates to set in motion constitutional amendments that would humble it.

In the case of *Cohens* v. *Virginia* (1821), the Court ran headlong into these aroused champions of states' rights, and Marshall made the most of the opportunity to put down the Court's critics. The facts were these: The Cohen brothers were convicted in the borough court of Norfolk, Virginia for selling lottery tickets in violation of state law. On the grounds that they had acted under a congressional law authorizing lotteries in the District of Columbia, they appealed directly to the Supreme Court on a writ of error. The first and most important question before the Court was whether it could maintain jurisdiction under Section 25 of the Judiciary Act. But behind this legal issue, said Marshall, there lay questions "of great magnitude" concerning the nature of the Union and of the position of the Supreme Court in the federal system. Bolstered by advice from the state legislature, counsel for Virginia used all the states' rights arguments that had accumulated since the Virginia and Kentucky Resolutions. The general doctrine of state sovereignty and the specific protection of the Eleventh Amendment prevented the Court from assuming jurisdiction, they concluded.

The Chief Justice's refutation of the states' rights contentions of Virginia was "one of the strongest and most enduring strands of that mighty cable woven by him to hold the American people together as a united and imperishable Nation," thought Albert Beveridge. And it rested on two premises: that the Constitution made a nation and that state jealousy perpetually threatened to unmake it. That nation is supreme, the objects for which it was created are supreme, and the departments of the federal government, while functioning to attain those objects, are supreme. The judicial department is no exception. Article III designates national law (i.e., questions where the rights of litigants depend on the construction of the Constitution or federal laws) as the Court's province, and in this area there can be no division—as Virginia maintained—between state and federal judiciaries. Appellate jurisdiction from state courts was a constitutional imperative when federal questions were involved, as established by Section 25 and by *Martin* v. *Hunter's Lessee.* The Eleventh Amendment, Marshall continued, was intended solely to prevent suits by individuals against states without their consent and it could not be used either to take questions of federal law from the purview of federal courts or "to maintain the sovereignty of a state from the degradation supposed to attend a compulsory appearance before the tribunal of the nation." Moreover, since Virginia had initiated the case against the Cohens and not the other way around, the Eleventh Amendment did not apply. After this stern lecture on the Court's duty to maintain national law, Marshall ruled for Virginia on the ground that the lottery statute applied only to the District of Columbia and was not intended to authorize the sale of tickets in Virginia. In short, that it was not a national law. This technical victory, far from placating Virginia, caused her to double her efforts against the Court. However, it was Marshall's "immortal national address" —not the states' rights complaints of Virginia—that history corroborated.

Three years later, in *Osborn* v. *Bank of the United States* (1824), Marshall was able to elaborate on the doctrines stated in the Bank and lottery cases. Ohio provided the occasion. In direct opposition to the *McCulloch* ruling, Ohio levied a tax on the Bank of the United States and, in open contravention of a circuit court injunction, collected it and refused to return the money. In January, 1821, Ohio outlawed the Bank entirely. The Bank turned to the Court for the enforcement of its rights, reviving the old questions of its constitutionality and its immunity from state taxation and raising the new one of whether the Bank would be given legal remedies sufficient to maintain its constitutional ground. The Chief Justice (with Justice Johnson in dissent) reaffirmed the Bank's constitutionality, voided the Ohio law, and gave the nation a new lecture on constitutional nationalism. By upholding the charter provision giving the Bank access to the federal courts, Marshall added substantially to the Bank's arsenal of legal weapons against state opposition. He further diminished the Eleventh Amendment (a process he had started in the Cohens case) by holding that it did not bar the Bank's suit against Osborn since the name of the state of Ohio did not appear on the record. Much more important than this interpretation of the Eleventh Amendment, which in fact was abandoned in *Ex parte Ayers,* 123 U.S. 443 (1887), was Marshall's ruling that agents of the state are personally liable for damages inflicted while implementing an unconstitutional statute.

But it was New York, not Ohio, steamboats, not banks, that provided Marshall with an opportunity to lay the last great foundation block of national power. *Gibbons* v. *Ogden* (1824) originated in a series of acts dating back to 1787. The New York state legislature had granted to the Fulton-Livingston steamboat interests the exclusive right of steam navigation on state waters, including the adjoining coastal waters and the Hudson River between New York and New Jersey. There had been several efforts to break the monopoly, but these were defeated in the state courts. The last challenge came from Thomas Gibbons, who had started a competing steamboat line. Gibbons was enjoined by Aaron Ogden, who sailed under license from the Livingston monopoly, and in 1820, the New York Court of Errors sustained the injunction. Gibbons then took his case to the Supreme Court. He argued against the monopoly on the grounds that the New York act which had given the company its exclusive rights conflicted with the federal Coasting License Act of 1793 and with the commerce clause of the Constitution (which gave Congress the right to regulate interstate commerce). For the first time the Court had a chance to clarify the meaning of the commerce clause and to coordinate federal and state power in this vital area. The immediate economic issue was hardly less important than the constitutional one. By the time the case was argued, three states had passed retaliatory statutes against New York and several others had begun the practice of granting steamboat monopolies. Such practices threatened to fractionalize national commerce and retard the use of new transportation—the steamboat in 1824, perhaps the railroad six years later.

In his opinion, Marshall began by speaking deferentially of the state court whose decision he was about to reverse; he then turned to the meaning of the commerce clause, and by extension to the meaning of all the enumerated powers in Article I, Section 8. The "well-settled rule" for their interpretation, asserted Marshall (though in fact the question had not previously come before the Court), was to construe the enumerated powers "by the language of the instrument which confers them, taken in connection with the purposes for which they were conferred." The powers granted in Article I, Section 8, were plainly stated: they were intended for the "general advantage" of the American people. The inexorable conclusion, therefore, was that "the sovereignty of Congress, though limited to specified objects, is plenary as to those objects."

Marshall vitalized enumerated powers in the *Gibbons* case in the same way he went beyond them to implied powers in *McCulloch* v. *Maryland*—by interpreting the Constitution according to the potent doctrine of national supremacy. Just how effective this approach was became clear when it was applied to the commerce clause. Commerce is not, as counsel for the state insisted, mere "interchange of commodities"; it includes "every species of commercial intercourse" among the states, said Marshall. And "among" means "intermingled with," which in turn means that the power of Congress over commerce does not stop at state boundaries but "may be introduced into the interior." And the power to "regulate"? Like other powers vested in Congress, it is "complete in itself, may be exercised to its utmost extent, and acknowledges no limitations other than are prescribed in the Constitution." The "sole restraints" against an abuse of this power, Marshall added (with an uncharacteristic nod to popular democracy), are the "wisdom and discretion of Congress" and the power of the vote.

Three possibilities were open to the Court in ruling on state authority in the area of commerce. The first, urged by Webster and closest to Marshall's concept of national power, was that the grant of power to Congress automatically and totally prohibited state legislatures from touching upon interstate commerce—at least its "higher branches." Less drastic was the proposition permitting states to legislate in areas of interstate commerce until Congress legislated on the same subject, at which time the state acts would give way. The third alternative, a refinement of the second, allowed state regulations of commerce to exist concurrently with those of Congress unless there was a direct and substantial conflict between the two, in which case the state act would give way. Extreme nationalists liked the first solution, and states' righters might be persuaded to take the third, for want of something better.

Marshall's opinion was an intricate blend of decisiveness and calculated vagueness that occupied solid nationalist ground, placated both extremes, and left the Court room to make future adjustments. (The complex story of what those adjustments have been is nicely summarized by George L. Haskins, "Marshall and the Commerce Clause of the Constitution," in W. Melville Jones, ed., *Chief Justice John Marshall,* 1956.) He accepted the third alternative—the one least offensive to the states—but in applying it added the nationalistic substance of the second. This he did by a broad reading of the federal Coasting License Act of 1793, under which Gibbons was licensed. Though the act merely required federal licensing of vessels engaged in the coastal trade, Marshall held that it was a national guarantee against state interference in interstate commerce. He then found the New York monopoly statute in conflict with this act and voided it. In his argument, however, Marshall hinted that the grant to Congress of commerce power might have been sufficient to void the state act even without an actual conflict.

The consequences were as profound as the intellectual footwork was dazzling. For the opinion disrupted an unpopular monopoly, prevented state fragmentation of commerce, established a national unit for commercial activity, and kept the states from impeding new technology. Philosophically the result was resolutely national: interstate commerce was defined so broadly that, in the twentieth century, it was able to embrace the revolution in communications and transportation and also provide constitutional support for national welfare legislation. Just by legislating, Congress could claim the whole field of interstate commerce from the states at any time. And, if the interpretation of the licensing act was any precedent, a little legislation would go a long way. By implication, this broad approach to the commerce power would apply to the other enumerated powers as well.

Three years later the consolidating potential of the Gibbons ruling was made explicit in *Brown* v. *Maryland* (1827). A Maryland tax law requiring importers of out-of-state goods and other wholesale vendors to take out a state license was the point at issue in the case. Marshall's majority opinion, over the powerful dissent of Justice Thompson, struck down the law as a violation of the constitutional prohibition of state duties on imports, even those coming from sister states (an interpretation not warranted by the Constitution and later reversed by the Court). Marshall also voided the law as a violation by Maryland of Congress' power to regulate interstate commerce, despite the fact that Congress had not legislated on the subject. Here, the implications of the Gibbons opinion became clear—the commerce power was foreclosed to the states just because it had been given to Congress. Then, assuming the policy-making role which Congress had renounced, Marshall introduced his rule for demarcating state and national commerce powers: as long as imported goods remained in the "original package," they could not be taxed by the states.

A PHILOSOPHY OF NATIONAL POWER

At no time in its history was the Court so close to transcending the policy-making limitations of the judicial process as in the six years from 1819 through 1824. This was largely due, as Holmes has suggested, to a happy combination of circumstances following the War of 1812. Congress, the executive, and the Court were inspired to come to accord by the formative possibilities of the age, and they were supported by a popular and progressive national sentiment. Indeed, Congress (as Curtis Nettels has reminded us in "The Mississippi Valley and the Constitution," December, 1924) paved the way for implied powers by acting on them. But neither Congress nor the executive was consistent enough in its practice or rational enough in its articulation to replace the Court as the authoritative interpreter of the Constitution. The absence of a well-defined party organization also left a vacuum that invited judicial activism. In addition, the series of related, comprehensive questions confronting the Court encouraged, even necessitated, an expansive exegesis that went far beyond the usual policy-making limits of case-controversy. In exploiting this potential, the Court was not circumscribed by precedents and, for the same reason, its work was precedent-making. Fortunately for the authority of its pronouncements, the Court did not have to originate *de novo* constitutional principles to fit the age. With the help of a brilliant bar led by William Pinkney, William Wirt, and Daniel Webster, it could and did draw on the nationalist political tradition rooted in the Revolution, potentially embodied in the Constitution, expounded by Hamilton, reflected in the policies of Washington and Adams and the dominant wing of the National Republican Party, and, as James Madison declared in 1830, "sustained by the predominant sense of the Nation."

John Marshall did not originate constitutional nationalism. Neither did he have to teach it to his colleagues (not even that assiduous Jeffersonian William Johnson, as Morgan's biography makes clear). More than historical legend admits, the nationalist victories of the great years were collective efforts. As Marshall himself indicated in 1819, "the opinion which is to be delivered as the opinion of the court is previously submitted to the consideration of all the judges; and if any part of the reasoning be disapproved, it must be so modified as to receive the approbation of all, before it can be delivered as the opinion of all." Yet it made a difference that John Marshall was there—and not, say, Spencer Roane as Jefferson wanted or Marshall's colleague Joseph Story—for his genius fitted the age. His natural leadership, coupled with the prerogatives of his office, enabled him as *primus inter pares* to guide the common nationalism of the judges over the hurdles of personal and tactical differences. His pragmatism helped him appreciate the needs of the moment, his conservatism to express those needs authoritatively. His capacity for lucid argument was as suited to the educative chore at hand as his stately rhetoric was to the profundity of the issues.

In its greatest national moments, the Court was represented by John Marshall. His separate decisions, taken collectively, amount to a unified and persuasive treatise on— if not a philosophy of—constitutional nationalism. Each opinion performed a special function in his exposition; all had nationalism and moral didacticism in common. Repetition and anticipation were his methods. Thus, while expounding implied powers in *McCulloch* v. *Maryland,* Marshall explored the principle of national supremacy that would vitalize the enumerated powers in *Gibbons* v. *Ogden.* In the *Cohens* opinion, he replied to criticism of the *McCulloch* ruling and reasserted the axioms of *Martin* v. *Hunter's Lessee.* At the same time, he anticipated the *Gibbons* decision by alluding to the supremacy of granted powers and to the idea of commerce as a national activity. *Brown* v. *Maryland* explored the theory set forth in the Gibbons decision—that the regulation of commerce belongs exclusively to Congress—and added the commerce clause to implied powers as a judicial weapon against state taxation of national business. Each decision turned on judicial discretion and strengthened judicial authority, yet perpetuated the myth of judicial modesty. None precluded flexibility of interpretation by future Courts. At the same time, the whole production bristled with Augustan rhetoric and moral imperatives: the nationalist doctrines which the Chief Justice liked were "part of our history," "self-evident" and "universally understood," doctrines which "the good sense of the public has pronounced," "the people have declared," and "America has chosen." The Court, Marshall insisted, had only to heed and then pronounce these verities of American experience.

Marshall's protestations of judicial passivity should not

obscure the emphatic shift in constitutional law wrought by his Court. In the first place, he assured that the Constitution would be sufficiently flexible to keep abreast of historical change. That it evolved through judicial processes rather than by formal amendment, as the Framers had planned, was scarcely less important. This was the large meaning of judicial review—the meaning that was not understood at Philadelphia. By the Court's power of interpretation, the compromises, deliberate obscurities, and convenient silences of the Constitution, as well as the unresolved tension between national and state power, fell into the background. Gone was the earlier image of the Constitution as an "accommodating system," as a "work of compromise," in Justice William Paterson's words. Marshall's vision of the "spirit and true meaning of the Constitution," tidied up the clutter of history. Through a clear and certain and supreme Constitution, the American people had spoken. Union was hypostatized into Nation; the government of limited authority, so much a part of colonial and revolutionary constitutionalism, became a government of sufficient power. The Constitution became the symbol of that Nation and the source of its vitality— a living, dynamic organism, based, as Nathan Dane had hoped in 1789, "on open manly principles."

Scarcely any political question arises in the United States that is not resolved, sooner or later, into a judicial question.

ALEXIS DE TOCQUEVILLE (1835)

THREE

Capitalism and the Marshall Court: The Uses of Power

In shaping constitutional law to meet the economic needs of the new nationalism, the Marshall Court implicitly recognized that the possession of constitutional power is inseparable from its use. The Court, content for practical reasons to act as the impartial expounder of a certain Constitution, never acknowledged that in deciding questions of constitutional law, it frequently made economic policy. Critics like Jefferson and John

Taylor, and astute observers like De Tocqueville, were more specific. And in the last quarter of the nineteenth century, judicial realists (Eugene V. Rostow tells the story well in "The Realist Tradition in American Law" in Arthur S. Schlesinger, Jr., and Morton White, eds., *Paths of American Thought,* 1963) rediscovered what the early critics knew: that "official" explanations of decision-making—such as the intent of the Framers or the eternal verities of natural law discovered through legal science—did not explain very much. Influenced by Darwinian science, Oliver Wendell Holmes (*Common Law,* 1881) and other pioneers tended to be skeptical of absolutes, to respect facts, and to appreciate the organic nature of things. They concluded that law, through the fallible person of the judge, was rooted in experience.

When historians looked at the Court realistically (as James Bradley Thayer did in his pioneering classic, "The Origin and Scope of the American Doctrine of Constitutional Law," 1893), they discovered its policy-making attributes. When they looked closer (as Corwin did in "The Basic Doctrine of American Constitutional Law," 1914), they recognized that the policy made by the antebellum Court was largely economic. What was not—and still is not—clear was how the function of economic policy-making fit into the overall scheme of judicial government. At one extreme, the socialist historian Gustavus Myers (*History of the Supreme Court,* 1912) accused the justices of conspiring with an exploitative capitalist elite against the democratic portion of the people. Louis Boudin (in *Government by Judiciary,* 1932) made the same charge twenty years later with more scholarship and less doctrine. Both Myers and Boudin assumed that the justices made policy at will with no regard for the legal rules of the game. On the other hand, in *The Supreme Court in United States History,* the work which set the dominant tone for subsequent historiography, Charles Warren acknowledged the economic influence of the Marshall Court but considered it less important than the Court's formal role as interpreter of the Constitution. He made no effort to explain the close relationship between law and economic development.

To separate law and economics for purposes of analysis may be necessary; to emphasize the former, as Warren did, because of the scope and endurance of the Marshall Court's constitutional decisions may be justifiable. Yet the complementarity of constitutional law and capitalism was too great to be accidental. The effect of law on economics is too powerful to be dismissed as a mere by-product of the search for legal truths. Still, there is little evidence that the Court cynically abandoned the limitations of its legal character to reach economic ends. There is even less evidence for—and much against—the theory of a conspiracy between the Court and economic interest groups. An account was (and still is) needed that would document and explain the substantial, inseparable, deliberate, yet unconspiratorial relationship between American capitalism and the Marshall and Taney Courts, an account that would evaluate the statesmanship of the Supreme Court in light of its simultaneous influence on American law and American economic development.

Such a synthesis gradually began to take shape; it presently constitutes one the most promising tendencies in constitutional historiography. Max Lerner's "The Supreme Court and American Capitalism" (March, 1933) was a notable early effort to abandon the conspiracy view of the Court for a broader cultural approach to judicial history. Following Lerner's essay, and like it drawing insight from the economic battles of the New Deal Court, came three distinguished works. Carl Swisher's 1935 biography *Roger B. Taney* (in fact a history of the Taney Court) treated the economic basis of judicial statesmanship frankly and analytically. Frankfurter's *The Commerce Clause under Marshall, Taney, and Waite* (1937) and Benjamin Wright's *Contract Clause of the Constitution* (1938) revealed the extent to which two key clauses of the Constitution could, under constructive interpretation by the Court, shape economic history. And the recent analysis of *Fletcher* v. *Peck* by C. P. Magrath (in *Yazoo: Law and Politics in the New Republic: Fletcher* v. *Peck,* 1966) illustrates, perhaps better than anything else, the subtle yet pervasive way in which interest groups used the Court to realize their economic goals. A social-economic history of the Court which weaves these various strands of scholarship into a comprehensive whole remains to be written. But Hurst's previously mentioned *Law and the Conditions of Freedom in the Nineteenth-Century United States* (1956) provides a conceptual basis on which such a work could rest.

To explain the legal-economic nexus in the Marshall and Taney period, then, one might begin with Max Lerner's observation—extrapolated from Holmes, refined by Corwin, and conceptualized by Hurst: "Between our business enterprise and our judicial power there is the unity of an aggressive and cohesive cultural pattern." The cultural proposition uniting law and economics (and much else in the nineteenth century) was the conviction that the individual was the *raison d'être* of civil society and the agent of national progress. And the vitalizing force behind creative individuals and the measure of social status was private property. Property, Chancellor Kent declared in the tradition of Locke, Blackstone, and Madison, was "inherent in the human breast." It was provided by God to lift men from sloth and stimulate them to display "the various and exalted powers of the human mind." (Or, as Francis Lieber put it, "Man yearns to see his individuality represented and reflected in the acts of his exertions—in property.") This impulse, continued Kent, "pervades the foundations of social improvement" and is the wellspring of civilization and the vehicle for national greatness. National advancement, both functionally and ideologically, was inseparable from the dynamics of economic individualism. If progress depended on the creative individual, it followed that government was obliged to foster the growth of these individual forces; the heritage of colonial mercantilism supported the conclusion.

For those who took on the responsibility of making government serve national progress by promoting individualism, there were complications. And contrary to the opinion of some historians, agreement on Lockean premises and the morality of individual enterprise did not produce a social, economic, or cultural consensus. The rich and varied economic landscape of the nineteenth century encouraged some to pursue Utopia through agriculture, others through shipping or manufacturing. Still others turned to selling, to finance, or to the professions. Within these groups were further divisions: rich-poor, free-slave, established-aspiring, creditor-debtor, corporation-individual. According to its own lights and in proportion to its strength, each group competed for nature's bounties and for the government assistance in exploiting them, to which it felt entitled. Self-interest forged these diverse groups into two amorphous and shifting cultural coalitions—the agrarian-minded and the commercial-minded (to use the apt phraseology of Lee Benson). Neither had the monopoly on devotion to national union. Each tended to view itself as the best hope of American civilization and each demanded that the Court sanction its own interpretation of the Constitution. The definition of constitutional power, then, was inseparable from considerations of economic policy. In shaping economic history as well as constitutional law, the Court could cement—or disrupt—the Union and shape national character.

The economic strategy of the Marshall Court was to attach the interests of powerful economic groups to the idea of national government. At the same time, the Court attempted to unleash the consolidating forces of interstate commerce by making constitutional law serve national capitalism. The preference was deliberate but not conspiratorial. It followed in the tradition of nationalist statesmanship since the Revolution. And the justices no less than other men of the age—perhaps more, since they came from the socially and educationally advantaged (see John Schmidhauser, "The Justices of the Supreme Court: A Collective Portrait," February, 1959)—imbibed the heady draught of nineteenth-century economic individualism. As practicing lawyers, most of them had associated with the dominant sector of the business community. As judges, they came easily to the conclusion that what helped the venturesome entrepreneur also helped the general welfare, and they worked consistently to translate nineteenth-century notions of economic man into legal rules that would maximize economic activity. When the Court had to choose among the economic interests competing for favor, the most broad-based and dynamic received priority. The Court attended, therefore, more to agrarian capitalism than subsistence agriculture, more to corporate business than domestic producers, more to the rich than the poor, and more to the freeman than the slave. And when confronted with the conflicting demands of agrarian capitalism based on states' rights, on one hand, and national, commercial capitalism, on the other, the Court gave preference to the latter as the more essential to national union.

THE MARSHALL COURT, STATE POWER, AND AGRARIAN CAPITALISM

There were few aspects of the Court's work that did not provide an occasion for buttressing the forces of capitalism. Even the consolidation of its own power held potential advantages for the business community. As the highest legal authority in the land, the Court could, as the *North American Review* assured its readers in 1828, put national law on a "steady and regular foundation." It was exactly this body of certain and uniform law, free from local and state idiosyncrasies, that expanding business needed. (As Daniel Webster advised Justice Story: "It is a great object to settle the concerns of the community; so that one may know what to depend on.") Viewed in this light, even the routine cases constituting most of the Court's work— like those concerned with revenue bonds, salvage, maritime insurance, land titles, liens, bills and notes, agency, patents, and corporate law—were means of facilitating and nationalizing economic activity.

The great nationalist decisions of the Marshall Court originated in economic conflict; the national powers established by those decisions were designed to promote national capitalism. The *McCulloch* decision, decided in favor of the largest corporation and most powerful monopoly in the country, underwrote a national system of internal improvements. If Congress had followed through, the system would have revolutionized national commerce. The *Gibbons* decision, in behalf of a national business community, gave Congress the constitutional power to make laws promoting commercial unity.

The Marshall Court's most direct and effective contribution to a national economy, however, was its curtailment of state power; here the Court plainly showed its preference for interstate capitalism and its skepticism of legislative democracy. To appreciate the Court's action, one must understand the extent of political and economic competition existing between state and nation in the early national period. State politics— through the expansion of suffrage, the multiplication of elective offices, and the development of party organization—led the way toward popular democracy. State government was the main source of legislative activity and administrative innovation. And it was to the states, not the federal government, that most of the responsibility for encouraging enterprise fell. They responded with an amazing range of legislation which included grants of incorporation, preferential tax policies, direct state investment (when the private sector lagged), and even outright state ownership. State regulation of wages, prices, and quality of goods and services presupposed that all this economic activity served the public good. But in carrying out these commercial responsibilities the states could and did inconvenience powerful segments of the business community—by restricting private property and by favoring local over national business interests. In addition, states' rights philosophy became the refuge for groups which lacked access to national power and therefore opposed its exercise for the benefit of others.

Given the assumption that government should serve economic enterprise, it was inevitable that state and nation would compete for the lion's share of the responsibility. This struggle was a basic theme in American history from the confederation period to World War II. State mercantilism was supported by a tradition rooted in colonial history, by its capacity to accommodate a variety of local interests, and by its advantageous association with popular democracy. On the other hand, national mercantilism, which favored interstate capital, was more congenial to American economic development and to dreams of national strength and glory. And if it was removed a step from grass-roots democracy, it was for that reason a more likely source of long-term, rational economic planning. Contemporaries saw the distinctions and, for a wide range of motives in which self-interest blends indistinguishably with idealism, took sides.

The Court was no exception, and, as constitutional arbiter of the federal system, it was able to influence the outcome of the political-economic struggle. That the Marshall Court would favor national mercantilism was soon very clear. In consolidating its own power, it had come down hard on both state legislatures and state courts. The concomitant effect (some said the primary motive) of judicial decisions expanding national power was to curb state mercantilism. *McCulloch* v. *Maryland* boldly encroached on the state power to tax and gave preferential treatment to a national corporation competing against state institutions. The *Gibbons* decision undid state promotional activity on behalf of state-based enterprise and gave Congress the authority to overrule state legislation in the area of interstate commerce. *Brown* v. *Maryland* added a further judicial barrier to state taxation and economic regulation (to the great pleasure of the interstate import merchants of Baltimore).

To serve national capitalism effectively the Court still needed a means of curtailing state interference in the rights of private property. For this, Marshall singled out Article I, Section 10, of the Constitution, which prohibited the states from emitting "bills of credit," passing ex post facto laws, and, most important of all, from "impairing the obligation of contracts." In addition, the quasi-legal doctrine of vested rights—a combination of Locke, natural rights, common law, and popular respect for property—was available to the Court. This doctrine upheld the individual's right to acquire, use, and enjoy the full returns of his property; even without specific constitutional prohibitions the legislatures were not to encroach on this special province. The Court had tried both approaches against the states but, before 1801, had explored neither fully. The achievement of the Marshall Court was to forge this inheritance into what Edward Corwin called, in his article of the same name, "the basic doctrine of American constitutional law" and to use it against any state interference with private property that retarded national capitalism.

It was no surprise that the Court began formulating this "basic doctrine" in behalf of agrarian capitalism. America, after all, started its capitalist career with the public domain. From the first, American law had encouraged those involved in land speculation, and it was assumed that the Supreme Court would not only continue but extend this legal benevolence. The land speculators among the Framers had made sure that land disputes would be decided by the Supreme Court rather than the Senate. The Federalist Party relied on the federal courts to support speculative land schemes and, during the short-lived Judiciary Act of 1801, removed cases on land titles from state to federal courts. (Kathryn Turner gives specifics in "Federalist Policy and the Judiciary Act of 1801," January, 1965). As far as the Supreme Court was concerned, such faith was not entirely unwarranted: from 1789 to the Civil War, many of the Justices had been associated in their pre-Court careers with the great national pastime of land speculation and they might, therefore, be sympathetic to those still engaged in it.

Fletcher v. *Peck* (1810), a model case study in the relationship of politics, economics, and constitutional law, called the Court into action (see Magrath's *Yazoo: Law and Politics in the New Republic*). The Georgia legislature set things in motion in 1795 when it granted 35 million acres, the so-called Yazoo lands, to four private land companies at the bargain price of less than one and one-half cents per acre. It was soon discovered that all but one of the legislators voting for the bill had been bribed and that many other officials—including two United States senators, the district attorney for the state, a judge of the Superior Court of Georgia, a federal district judge, and Justice James Wilson of the Supreme Court—were implicated in the fraud. The guilty legislators were straightway returned to private life. In 1796, the new legislature repealed the original grant and voided all property rights attached to it. And to emphasize the point, the legislature publicly burned the original act and expunged all traces of it from state records. While the repeal was in progress, however, the land companies sold portions of the grant to innocent third parties—one being a well-organized interest group called the New England Mississippi Company, which purchased 11 million acres. John Peck of Boston, a director of this company, sold a small portion of his 600,000 acre investment to Robert Fletcher of New Hampshire. Fletcher then sued Peck in the federal circuit court in Massachusetts for breach of warranty of title, i.e., for selling him land which he did not rightfully possess. As Magrath proves beyond doubt, both the initial transaction and the suit were feigned to circumvent the Eleventh Amendment and bring the constitutionality of the Georgia repeal before the Supreme Court. This became obvious when Fletcher appealed the circuit court decision which completely validated his title to the Yazoo land.

The issues, more complex than the obvious chicanery makes them appear, called for a response to a basic problem in nineteenth-century political economy. For, in repealing the grant, the state legislature had performed its mercantilist duty. To deny it this power, in the face of an obvious fraud, would scuttle the public welfare and invite special interests to invade state legislatures—a practice for which they hardly needed encouragement. On the other hand, giving state legislatures an unlimited right to revoke previous grants might jeopardize confidence in all public grants and the private contracts based upon them; this, in turn, would discourage investment and thwart creative enterprise. A middle course would be to designate the Supreme Court as the judge of when and what grants should be voided. But to do so, Marshall saw, would plunge the Court into a tangled jungle of interest-group politics, where there were no clear legal paths to follow.

The Court wisely settled this question of judicial capacity and simultaneously advanced the cause of agrarian capitalism. By focusing only on the question of private contract between Fletcher and Peck (by a literal interpretation of the pleadings, in other words), Marshall was able to declare that the only question before the Court was one of "title." And, he added,

"It would be indecent in the extreme, upon a private contract between two individuals, to enter into an inquiry respecting the corruption of the sovereign power of a State." Legislative motive was not an area in which the Court was willing or equipped to adjudicate, a position which subsequent Courts have frequently affirmed. On the other hand, the question of whether a state legislature could "annihilate" a bona fide contract between two private citizens and "destroy the presumption of property thus held" was an issue the Court could answer. That the people of Georgia had been defrauded of several million acres of public land was no business of the Court but a matter between them and their agents.

In denying Georgia the right to void a private contract, the Chief Justice turned to the clause in Article I, Section 10, of the Constitution which prohibited the states from impairing "the obligation of contract." But there were some embarrassing problems. Very little had been said about the clause either at the Constitutional Convention or in the state ratifying conventions. What had been said linked the contract clause and the others in Section 10 with the problem of state regulation of the currency. On the meaning of "contract," the overwhelming opinion of those who had any opinion at all (as B. F. Wright's *Contract Clause of the Constitution* establishes) was that it was limited to private contracts between A and B and not to public ones between the state and private parties—the case in Georgia's grant to the land companies. Opposed to this confining view were scattered private statements, before and after 1787, asserting that "contract" embraced public charters and grants. The most powerful of these was Hamilton's private legal brief of 1796 arguing that the Georgia rescinding act (the one before the Court) came within the prohibition imposed by the contract clause. The circuit court's decision in *Vanhorne's Lessee v. Dorrance* (1795), which used the contract clause along with vested rights to void a legislative act taking private property, was the closest thing to legal precedent available.

Sensing the weakness of relying entirely on the contract clause, Marshall approached the subject cautiously through the doctrine of vested rights, which he had broached before in his mandamus opinion. "It may well be doubted whether the nature of society and of government does not prescribe some limits to the legislative power. . . . ," Marshall observed. And, without citing any precedent or referring to the Philadelphia or ratifying conventions, he went on to declare that the original grant by the Georgia legislature was a contract within the meaning of Section 10 and that the rescinding act was an unconstitutional impairment of it. The closest Marshall came to a justification was his assertion that such an interpretation was not precluded by the words of the clause and that the "sentiment" of the Framers was in favor of protecting property from state "passions." To prop up his assertions (or perhaps to divert attention from them), Marshall declared that the ex post facto provision of Section 10 would also have voided the act—conveniently forgetting that *Calder* v. *Bull* (1798) had limited the ex post facto clause to criminal matters. Apparently, he still had some doubts about the contract clause, for when he finally returned to it in his opinion, he linked the clause firmly to vested rights, voiding the Georgia rescinding act "either by general principles which are common to our free institutions, or by the particular provisions of the Constitution of the United States." Justice Johnson, preferring not to rely on those "particular provisions," based his concurrence entirely on vested rights.

The Yazoo opinion readied the contract clause for use as a constitutional weapon against state interference with property rights, expanded the meaning of property to include the right to acquire as well as possess, and advertised the judicial process to future capitalists as an implement of economic policy-making.

Whether the decision fulfilled Madison's expectations in *Federalist* No. 44, that the contract clause would "inspire a general prudence and industry, and give a regular course to the business of society," is less certain. Perhaps it did establish a "regular course." State grants were contracts with the Court's imprimatur upon them. The state and its people were forewarned that they would be stuck with bad bargains, and businessmen knew where they stood. But whether the speculation and struggle for legislative favors which the opinion encouraged did further "prudence and industry" is more doubtful. In any case, the opinion was in good nineteenth-century style. It was revealing that Jefferson's appointee and friend William Johnson should make the point. Property once granted to a man, he wrote, "becomes intimately blended with his existence, as essentially as the blood that circulates through his system." So the very "reason and nature of things" prohibited the state from revoking such a grant.

New Jersey v. *Wilson* (1812) was the first in a long series of contract decisions which came in the wake of the *Fletcher* opinion. In 1758, the colonial government of New Jersey had granted tax exemption to certain lands belonging to the Delaware Indians. In 1801, the Delawares sold their lands and moved on to New York; in 1804, the state repealed the tax exemption. The purchasers of the Indian lands claimed these tax privileges, arguing that the state repeal violated the contract made with the Indians and was void under the contract clause. In his opinion, Marshall ignored the importance to the state of its power to tax land as well as the unique nature of the tax exemption in question; if he had dealt with these matters, the burden of proof would have been on the speculators. Since the state had not required a surrender of tax exemption as a condition in permitting the Indians to sell, Marshall ruled, the favored position became attached to the land and was passed on with the sale. The excessive zeal of the Court in promoting land speculation should not be obscured by the fact that New Jersey disregarded the decision and continued to collect taxes for some sixty years.

In a series of decisions following the *New Jersey* case, the Court managed, simultaneously, to assert the supremacy of national law, stabilize land titles, and consolidate the interests of large speculators. In *Fairfax's Devisee* v. *Hunter's Lessee* (1813), Justice Story for the Court used the Treaty of 1794 to void Virginia's confiscation of Tory lands during the Revolution, and he upheld the right, contested by Virginia, of an alien to inherit land. Besides supporting national law, the decision validated the claims of speculators to nearly 300,000 acres of rich land. (Marshall had been one of these so he did not sit in the case.) In 1815, Virginia was again put in her place and again it was by Justice Story, who was becoming as infamous in that state as Marshall. The colony of Virginia had granted lands for the support of the Episcopal Chuch; after the disestablishment of religion, the state repealed these grants. Fearing that this act would "uproot the very foundations of almost all the land titles in Virginia," Story again fused the contract clause and vested rights to strike it down in *Terrett* v. *Taylor* (1815).

Green v. *Biddle* (1823) climaxed a series of decisions in which the contract clause advanced agrarian capitalism. Better than any, it laid bare the undemocratic consequences of the Court's preferences. The case arose from a 1791 agreement between Virginia and Kentucky (at the time of the latter's separation from Virginia) in which Kentucky promised not to invalidate titles to land held under Virginia law. Kentucky pioneers—and most of the legal profession—did not understand the intricacies and uncertainties of Viriginia land law or appreciate the virtues of absentee ownership. Assuming that they held valid titles, they took up land and labored to improve it only to find in many instances that they owned neither the land nor their improvements. Without money or connections, they were prey for unscrupulous speculators and lawyers. Kentucky attempted to ease the plight of these settlers with a series of laws providing that no claimant under Virginia title could take land until he had reimbursed the original settler for improvements made on it. The constitutionality of these laws was contested in *Green* v. *Biddle*. The specific questions facing the Court were whether the 1791 agreement between Virginia and Kentucky was a contract within the meaning of the Constitution, and if so, whether the Kentucky claimant laws violated it.

The case had been argued three times, and, by 1823, it had become a rallying point for states' rights and anti-Court forces in the South and West. The Court was sensitive to their opposition but not deterred. It invalidated the Kentucky laws on the ground that they violated the original agreement between the states and thus the contract clause of the Constitution—

this despite the fact that there had been no talk in or out of the Constitutional Convention about the contract clause being extended to agreements between sovereign states. Nor was the Court deterred by the fact that the Virginia land law which it upheld was notoriously irrational, inefficient, and unjust. To the great pleasure of Jefferson, Justice Johnson revived his democratic sentiments and entered a strongly worded separate opinion, which was, in all but name, a dissent.

The Court (as Paul Gate's "Tenants of the Log Cabin" [June, 1962] demonstrates) did not have the last word, however. The squatters were not persuaded by judicial sincerity and they refused to obey the decision. (We are answerable, declared Justice Washington, "to God, our consciences, and our country.") And state authorities, who were convinced because of the absence of three judges and Johnson's "dissent" that the decision had been rendered by a minority of three, backed up the squatters. Indeed, more effective claimant laws were passed and enforced, setting a pattern for other western states. In Congress, meanwhile, Kentucky joined other states that were disaffected by judicial conservative-nationalism in a concerted move to curb the Court's power.

Running parallel to and complementing the contract decisions were a series of lesser known cases which also helped the man who had everything—and wanted more. *Huidekoper's Lessee* v. *Douglass* (1805) led the way. Pennsylvania had passed a law in 1792 prohibiting land speculation and absentee ownership by making title contingent on occupancy. (The law was directed particularly against the Holland Land Company, which claimed several hundred thousand acres of state land.) Reversing the decision of the state supreme court, Marshall interpreted the ambiguously worded statute out of existence. He validated the Holland Company claims by holding that the grantee by warrant had title even if he didn't occupy the land, providing he tried to do so and was prevented by enemies of the country, i.e., the Indians. Twenty-five years later the conservative *American Quarterly Review* praised the Court for rising up "in its power and independence" to put the pretentious "*Squatters*" in their place. Another quarter century later the

Taney Court, which had presumably made peace with American democracy, resuscitated *Huidekoper's Lessee* to confirm the titles of speculators in California lands.

In the meantime the Adams-Onís Treaty of 1819 provided some fertile opportunities for the big investor. Under that treaty, the United States agreed to recognize land grants made by the King of Spain prior to January 24, 1818. While ratification was pending, however, a spate of hastily manufactured and fraudulent grants were made to American adventurers by Spanish officials. To validate their precarious titles, these speculators turned to the federal courts. The Court accommodated them in a series of decisions (see *United States* v. *Arrendondo, 1832*, for example) by applying the principle and spirit of *Fletcher* v. *Peck* and refusing to look behind the face of the grant for fraud. "He who would controvert a grant executed by the lawful authority," as the Court put it in the *Clarke* case in 1834, ". . . takes upon himself the burden of showing . . . that the transaction is tainted with fraud." Armed with this presumption of legality, speculators made good their claims to several million acres from the Louisiana Purchase and the Florida and Mexican cession territories.

The Supreme Court, it seems fair to say, lived up to its advance billing as a friend of those seeking capital gains in the land market. But in view of nature's plenitude and the prevailing assumption that the law would help those who helped themselves, the preferences of the Court were understandable —if not inevitable. No doubt the judges honestly believed that what helped Superintendent of Finance Robert Morris, President Washington, Justice Wilson, the Reverend Manasseh Cutler, Senator Daniel Webster, and General John C. Frémont (to mention a few prominent land investors) also helped the common people. What the multitudes who cleared the land and fought the Indians and nature thought about this trickle-down theory can only be surmised. One thing is certain: Enterprise in land whetted appetites, provided the financial base, and set the style for more dynamic forms of economic activity.

THE COURT AND CORPORATE CAPITALISM: MARSHALL'S PLAN

During the age of Marshall and Taney, no development was more significant in shaping the country than the rise of the business corporation. Not that the corporation was an American original. As early as the sixteenth century, the corporation had assumed its essential character, i.e., an association of private individuals for the accomplishment of private goals. (As a societal organization, like the guild or religious order, it ran even further back into Western history.) The corporate device was well known in both England and the Colonies in the seventeenth and eighteenth centuries, but it was employed almost exclusively as an instrument of political organization. Its application to business, and particularly to productive enterprise, was rare. In fact, throughout the eighteenth century hardly more than a dozen business corporations were chartered in England and, up through the Revolution, even fewer in the Colonies. Yet it was mainly as an instrument of economic activity that the corporation made its mark on American history. The adaptation of the politically-oriented corporate heritage to the economic exigencies of the American people was a major creative accomplishment of antebellum law—one in which the Supreme Court played an important role.

The combination of individual and associational features in the corporation made it ideally suited to nineteenth-century American ideas and needs. As De Tocqueville observed, the associational impulse pervaded the age. Associations of every degree—"moral, serious, futile, general or restricted, enormous or diminutive"—were applied by Americans to projects of every description—political, religious, educational, and economic. Far from contradicting the individualism of the age, the associational drive was a logical extension of it. If the individual was the agent of progress and individual accomplishment the measure of morality, it was only natural that individuals should join together for the more efficient accomplishment of their private goals. And nowhere was the collective impulse more appropriate than in the exploitation of nature.

Obviously, Americans made the connection. In 1780, the business corporation was almost unknown; by the end of the century, American states had chartered 310 corporations. To be sure, most of these were connected with turnpikes, bridges, and canals, but eight were in productive enterprises. Between 1800 and 1817, 1,794 more corporations were chartered, with a large proportionate increase of those engaged in production. By 1830, the New England states alone had established 1900 corporations, 600 of which were devoted to manufacturing and mining. Individual enterprises, copartnerships, and unincorporated joint stock companies continued to outnumber corporations. But before the end of the Taney period, the corporation had proved that it was the most viable, dynamic form of business organization.

There were other reasons—besides its congeniality to the individual-associational impulse—why the corporation was preferred to other forms of business organization as the vehicle for the economic revolution. Like these other devices, the corporation permitted the accumulation of capital from a broad base, which was especially important in a country without consolidated class wealth. It also permitted the centralized management of capital necessary for its efficient use. What made the corporation uniquely attractive to America, however, was that it was an ideal instrument by which government could perform its obligation to aid private enterprise. Given the individualism of the age and the manifestation of this individualism in associations, it was only logical for government to promote enterprise by aiding these associations. Indeed, as De Tocqueville brilliantly perceived, this was the only way a democratic government could act. To work through an aristocratic class was impossible since there was none. To bestow privileges on select individuals violated egalitarian principles. For government itself to take on economic enterprise too big for single individuals was impracticable—in view of the embryonic state of administrative techniques and the multiplicity of undertakings—and might threaten democracy with too much government. For government to give legal recognition, through the charter, to an association of private individuals, arming them with a portion of sovereign power and privilege, was a solution which satisfied both expediency and ideology.

The corporation, then, was a creation of the law. Before it could serve American economic needs, a body of legal principles to define and to guide it was needed. For this, American lawmakers could turn to the inherited body of corporate law as well as related principles from other legal fields. But the inheritance was only partly applicable to American circumstances. The corporate form had to be fitted into the federal system and the democratic polity. And further, this basically political device had to be transformed into an economic instrument that would serve the peculiar individual-oriented pattern of American economic life. It was this collision of legal tradition with the "pressure of new interests," as Roscoe Pound observed in his pioneering *The Formative Era of American Law* (1938), that provided the basis for a period of creative legal development. American lawmakers fused these elements into the most sophisticated body of corporation law in the Western world. (The legal story is told in E. M. Dodd's indispensable *American Business Corporations until 1860,* 1954.)

The Supreme Court was, of course, only one of several lawmaking agencies engaged in formulating corporate law. The legislative charter—granted at first by special acts for each corporation and, increasingly in the 1830's, by general statutes of incorporation—bestowed legal life on private associations, gave them power and rights, and imposed duties and obligations. With the exceptions of the first and second Banks of the United States, state legislatures, rather than Congress, granted these charters. Exactly how these new legal entities would function became apparent only in practice, and the job of filling in the interstices of statute law with essential detail was one the courts could perform well.

State judiciaries led the way in this creative enterprise. Beginning around the turn of the century, an ever-increasing body of state decisional law—on such matters as the internal government of the corporation, the transfer and sale of corporate shares, the nature of corporate contracts and property rights, and the liability of corporate agents, of shareholders for corporate debts, of the corporation itself for torts—made the corporation a workable business instrument. State courts also contributed to public corporation law by determining the relations of the corporation to legislative power. Among other things, they settled the doctrine of eminent domain and provided devices—the prerogative writs of mandamus and *ultra vires*—that could be used against a corporation exceeding or abusing its charter grant.

Through its diversity of citizenship jurisdiction and its broad powers in both law and equity, the Supreme Court was able to join with state courts in shaping the private law of corporations. Sometimes, as in Justice Story's opinion declaring the liability of corporations for contracts made by their agents (*Bank of Columbia* v. *Patterson's Administrator,* 1813), the Supreme Court showed the way. Sometimes it built onto or refined doctrines broached first in state courts, as in Story's exegesis of the distinction between public and private corporations (begun in *Terrett* v. *Taylor,* 1815, and expanded in his *Dartmouth College* opinion, 1819), or holding in *Wood* v. *Dummer* (1824) that the capital of a stock corporation is a trust fund for its creditors, or with the series of Supreme Court decisions defining the legal responsibilities of corporate agents. At other times, as in the area of tort liability of corporations, the Court (*Fowle* v. *Common Council of Alexandria,* 1830) merely recognized doctrines formulated in state courts. Occasionally the Supreme Court encroached on the jurisdiction of state courts to make its points. But most often it built on the creative efforts of the lower courts, using its high position to synthesize and expound the doctrines of state judges like John Bannister Gibson of Pennsylvania, Lemuel Shaw of Masachusetts, and Chancellor James Kent of New York.

It was as the interpreter of the Constitution and arbiter of federal power, however, that the Court left its real mark on corporate development. By virtue of these domains, the Court was able to define the legal status of the corporation and regulate corporate expansion across interstate lines and, at the same time, limit state control over economic behavior within state borders. In other words, the Court could influence the relationships between the corporation's private rights and its public responsibilities because it controlled governmental power. Not just the exploratory efforts of state courts in public law and inherited legal principles were involved in this process; so were the nineteenth-century notions of politics, economics, and morality. In making corporate law, the Court gradually fused these ingredients into an authoritative ideology—if not a philosophy, then at least the ground rules for free enterprise.

The decisive question was whether the corporation would derive its legal character from the individuals who comprised it or from the public power that created it. If the former, then the rights of private property could be attached to the corporation and cloak its operations. If the latter, government control over it as a predominantly public instrument would be implicit. In *Head* v. *Providence Insurance Co.* (1804), the Court grappled with this issue for the first time. Marshall's legal definition of the corporation clearly emphasized its public character and implied legislative dominance over it. The corporation, he declared, "is the mere creature of the act to which it owes its existence," and "all its powers" and the manner in which they may be used are determined by this act.

This definition corresponded historically to the mercantilist view of the corporation as basically an instrument for the accomplishment of public goals. It continued to make sense as long as corporate enterprise was predominantly in the public service—i.e., turnpikes, canals, hospitals, and the like. With its increased application to individual businesses and production, however, this quasi-public conception seemed less tenable. The Court began to shift its view of the corporation accordingly.

In *Bank of the United States* v. *Deveaux* (1809), which dealt with a corporation's right to sue in federal courts, the Court began the process of adjustment. The jurisdictional issue raised the question of corporate character again. As an abstract legal creature, the corporation was unknown to the Constitution or the Judiciary Act of 1789 and must, Marshall admitted, "be excluded from the courts of the Union." Only if the Court could look beyond the legal entity to the individuals involved could a jurisdictional accommodation be made. Marshall proceeded to turn this contingency into law. The corporation is, he repeated, an invisible, artificial creation of the law. But a corporation is also the individuals who comprise it. And although the citizenship of these members cannot make the corporations a citizen within the law, common sense and the common law make it clear, said Marshall, that these individuals do have legal rights which attach to the aggregate. The right to sue is one of them. Accordingly, either a federal or state corporation may sue in federal courts under the diversity of citizenship clause if its members are citizens of a state other than the party being sued.

The practice of determining jurisdiction by looking at the individuals behind the corporate name later proved unworkable and had to be abandoned, but its implications were large. For if the individual, private nature of the corporation might be emphasized for jurisdictional purposes, why not for the purpose of bestowing other private legal rights, such as the protection of corporate property from legislative encroachment? This possibility was explored in *Terrett* v. *Taylor* (1815). In that case, Story separated the public and private aspects of corporate character, which had been implicit in earlier cases, into two separate categories—public corporations and private corporations. This was a distinction not yet established in American law. The functional difference between the two categories had to do with legislative control over them. The charters of public corporations, conceded Story, might be modified "under proper limitations," but, according to his definition, this category included only "counties, towns, and cities." The property rights of private corporations—all the rest—were protected by both natural rights and constitutional law. The stage was now set for including the privileges granted by the government in charters under those property rights which could not be abridged by legislation. The drama, starring John Marshall with Joseph Story and Daniel Webster in supporting roles, was entitled *Dartmouth College* v. *Woodward* (1819).

The *College* case seemed unpromising material for the

cause of capitalism. The issue was whether the New Hampshire legislature could amend Dartmouth's charter (granted by George III in 1769) by increasing the number of trustees and making them appointees of the governor. This change was intended to transform the college into a state-controlled university. In the state superior court, Judge Richardson rejected arguments asserting that the legislature's act violated vested rights, the New Hampshire Constitution, and the contract clause of the United States Constitution. He ruled that the college was in fact a public corporation and therefore subject to state regulation in the public interest. The constitutional issues in the case came before the Supreme Court on a writ of error.

Marshall had promised "cautious circumspection" in dealing with such important matters but showed little in handing down one of his most audaciously creative opinions. The substance of Marshall's opinion was this: Dartmouth College is a "private eleemosynary institution" and therefore a private corporation. A charter to such a corporation is really a contract within the protection of the contract clause of the Constitution, and, therefore, the New Hampshire act amending the charter must be void. To arrive at this conclusion that private ("eleemosynary") and public ("civil") corporations ("institutions") differed in their subordination to legislative control, Marshall relied on Story's argument in *Terrett* v. *Taylor*. And Story, supported in turn by Bushrod Washington, spelled out the technicalities of the subject in a separate concurring opinion. But even with all this substantiation, the fact remained that the immunity of "private" corporations from legislative control had only a shaky foundation in Anglo-American law, and Marshall himself implied as much when he admitted Parliament's unlimited power to annul corporate rights.

The Chief Justice was also on dubious legal ground when he turned to the contract clause. It "can require no argument," he declared, to prove that a charter of a corporation (including presumably those issued by state legislatures) is a contract. But he was unable to cite conclusive precedents to back himself up —because there were none. In addition, he had to admit that the Framers had not exactly intended to include corporation charters under "contracts" in Article I, Section 10. But Marshall believed it was enough that such an interpretation fit the spirit of the Constitution and was not prohibited by it. Having hypothesized the rule, he then concluded that the case at hand was not so exceptional as to escape it.

The consequences of the Chief Justice's improvisations were great. Privately endowed educational corporations were now protected by law against state interference, and the legal future of private education in America was guaranteed. Furthermore, the new business corporations—and in 1819 there were about one thousand corporations for every fifty private educational ones—came under this protective blanket (thanks particularly to Justice Story's concurring opinion). State legislative charters creating corporations were now contracts within the meaning of Article I, Section 10, of the Constitution; once granted they could no longer be altered, even for the public good. Story introduced a modest note of judicial restraint in his concurring opinion by assuring the state that it had only to reserve the right to regulate explicitly in the charter. This softened the blow of the judicial curtailment but, given the vulnerability of legislatures to special interest pressures, hardly eliminated it. Assured of the stability of charter grants and strategically placed to exact choice ones, the private corporation was ready for business.

Dartmouth College v. *Woodward* was the first of three great pro-business, anti-state decisions of the 1819 term. The other two were *Sturges* v. *Crowninshield* and *McCulloch* v. *Maryland*. The latter, as we have already seen, served national commerce by legalizing the Second Bank of the United States, by providing constitutional power for federal internal improvements, and by curtailing state taxing powers. The *Sturges* case dealt with the constitutionality of a New York bankruptcy law. Coming as it did at the onset of a national depression, it was a subject of vital concern to the business community. Most people agreed that clear and equitable laws regulating bankruptcy were imperative in the new age of commerce; the question was whether these laws should be passed by Congress or by the states. Article I, Section 8, of the Constitution gave Congress the power to establish uniform bankruptcy laws for the nation, but Congress had not acted. Instead the states had assumed the legislative burden. The New York law before the Court was one such instance. Therefore, the Court's decision on the constitutionality of that law would affect the whole body of state regulation in the area of bankruptcy.

The New York legislation raised two questions: Did the constitutional grant vesting Congress with the power to establish national bankruptcy laws automatically prohibit state bankruptcy legislation? And, assuming it did not, what limitations did the contract clause of the Constitution impose on such state legislation? Marshall, who spoke for the Court, conceded that the states did have the power to pass bankruptcy laws in the absence of congressional legislation on the subject. But he had no intention of surrendering the Court's supervisory powers over such legislation, and he claimed such authority by virtue of Article I, Section 10, of the Constitution. The contract clause of that section prohibited the state from impairing the obligation of contract; applied to bankruptcy laws, this meant that the state could alter only the remedy for and not the substance of the contract. Turning to the New York law, Marshall found that it applied to contracts made before its passage, and for this reason he struck it down as a violation of the contract clause. Marshall's intent seems clear, but the impact of the decision was dissipated because its meaning was misunderstood. Those who listened most closely to Marshall's stern words on the contract clause assumed that the decision was a practical prohibition of all state bankruptcy laws. Others, including some of the justices, emphasized Marshall's doctrine of concurrent power and assumed that the opinion gave states wide discretion to pass bankruptcy laws so long as the laws applied to contracts made after the passage of the act. The country waited anxiously for clarification until *Ogden* v. *Saunders* in 1827.

The ambiguity of one decision should not detract from the unity of the Marshall Court's plan for American greatness. When one fits the political, economic, and legal pieces together, the plan emerges as a remarkable mosaic. Starting from the assumption that morality and capitalism are synonymous, the Marshall Court made the corporation the vehicle of capitalism by identifying it with the enterprising individual. And because the Court viewed the corporate charter as a private contract immune to legislative interference, the corporations were able to attract sufficient capital to develop new productive techniques and operate on a national scale. The Court then secured that national field of operations for the corporation by striking down state obstructions with constitutional nationalism. All the advantages of mercantilism, and none of its disabilities, were extended to the entrepreneurs who came forth. Implied powers meant that Congress could pass promotional legislation; actual practice assured that no national regulation would accompany this paternalism. Though the states were prevented from interfering with property, they were free, through the granting of corporate charters and other legislation, to subsidize enterprise. The legal foundation was being laid for the promotional, nonregulatory state of post-Civil War America.

Marshall and his colleagues on the bench expected great things from the unchained forces of capitalism. National commerce would obliterate sectionalism and, stimulated by self-interest, would forge lasting bonds of national union. The new conservative class of businessmen and lawyers who rose to guide the forces of capitalism would replace the vanishing gentleman ruler of the old republic and counterbalance the untrustworthy professional, democratic politician. Perhaps it was true, as Story and Webster allowed themselves to think, that once commerce was liberated by free trade, facilitated by uniform commercial law, and led by the new champions of *noblesse oblige,* it would transcend nationalism and establish the basis of a *pax Atlantica.*

RETREAT UNDER FIRE

Because of its timing, history had supported the Court's nationalism and tolerated its liberties with the Constitution of 1787. But after 1819, circumstances threatened to undo all that had formerly been encouraged. Panic and depression and the debates over slavery made it clear that beneath the mutual devotion to the Union there were profound sectional divisions over whether American culture should be agrarian or commercial. Contemporaries saw that the Court had put the Constitution on the side of commerce and proceeded to debate the cultural issue in terms of constitutional law—with the Court of John Marshall as the point of contention. For its last decade (1825–1835), the Court faced a hostile political and economic environment and determined enemies. Its less than successful response to the new age—in methods and substance of legal adjustments—and the decline of its institutional *élan* have led historians to modify earlier estimates of the Marshall Court drawn entirely from its golden days.

The allegations against the Court were sweeping. It had usurped an authority, the charge began, to determine the political balance of power in the federal system; this authority was not granted by the Constitution and, because of the prejudices of the justices, it would "be on the side of power and of the government which feeds them." By unauthorized judicial amendment, the Court undermined the constitutional system of limited government and dual federalism. (Jefferson described the process as "sapping and mining" and "twistification.") If, as John Taylor said in good anti-Federalist style, the state legislatures were "the people themselves," then the Court struck at democracy itself. Finally, the preference of the Court for corporate capitalism completed the indictment: the Court was in collusion with Hamilton's party, which had been trying since the Revolution to turn democratic government, rooted in state-based agrarianism, into an oligarchy ruled by a national, moneyed aristocracy.

However unfairly, the critics blamed John Marshall. By cunning and insinuation, they complained, he bewitched his weak-willed associates—including Republican appointees. He subverted the democratic procedures of the Court by eliminating separate opinions and usurped the prerogative of writing the Court's opinions himself. In short, he made the Court his own tool and used it to read Hamiltonian political and economic principles into constitutional law.

The assault on the Court was comprehensive. The *McCulloch* and *Cohens* opinions solidified the alliance in Virginia between the Old Republicans (typified by John Randolph) and nascent Southern sectionalists. This new conservative coalition, led by John Taylor and Spencer Roane, countered the Marshall Court's opinions with a war of words, elaborating its own doctrinal alternatives. In 1822, Jefferson pleaded with Justice William Johnson to break Marshall's hold on the Court and prevent the practice of "cooking up opinions in conclave" by reinstituting the practice of separate opinions. States in the South and West prepared to resist unpopular decisions while more permanent remedies against "judicial tyranny" were considered. There were numerous suggestions. Some thought the Senate should be made the supreme appellate court, others that the justices should have six-year terms like senators. And Congress actually considered requiring a majority of at least five of seven justices in constitutional decisions, or giving the Senate appellate jurisdiction in questions involving state sovereignty. Most serious was the effort to repeal or modify Section 25 of the Judiciary Act, since it could be done by legislative act rather than constitutional amendment. After 1828, the Jacksonian Democrats, who pledged to eradicate "neo-Federalism," were in office and even more drastic correctives seemed likely.

The Court did have its own enthusiastic supporters who rallied to its defense, especially in the Middle and Northern states. The "wise and the good and the elevated in society," as Story called the friends of the Court, had their own diagnosis of the nation's ills: the disease was Thomas Jefferson. His "loose and visionary" ideas, the charge went, were demagogic tools to gain popular power and gratify an insatiable ambition. He hated the Court because, in checking the "wild impulse of the moment," it curtailed his own power. And it was Jefferson who inspired and guided the assault on the judiciary. The destruction of the Court, its defenders firmly believed, was only the first step in a process that would end in subverting the Constitution itself. Across the nation, conservatives toasted John Marshall and mobilized to save the Court and constitutional Union.

The Court was saved, or rather saved itself. But it was not the "old Court" that survived. In the years between 1811 and 1823, that Court was the most stable in judicial history: there had not been a new justice since 1811 and together the justices had accumulated 123 years of experience by 1823. Mutual respect, communal living, congenial principles, and personal friendship held dissent to an insignificant minimum, bound the Court together as never before or since, and enabled it to exploit the opportunities for lawmaking in the postwar period.

The inevitable change began in 1823. Henry Brockholst Livingston died in that year and was replaced by Smith Thompson. Robert Trimble replaced Thomas Todd in 1826, only to be replaced himself three years later by President Jackson's appointee John McLean. Henry Baldwin's appointment in 1830 to fill the chair of Bushrod Washington was another blow to the old solidarity. In 1828 the selection of Richard Peters as Supreme Court reporter—against considerable opposition from the Court—added further to the disunity. Gone were the old camaraderie and accord, and gone too, in large part, was Marshall's unique position of power. As Donald Morgan's biography of Justice William Johnson shows, it was Johnson's determination to salvage a few Jeffersonian principles that brought the division into the open. During the ten years following 1823, Johnson wrote twenty-seven separate opinions, eighteen of which were dissents, and the new justices followed his example. The Chief Justice was still intellectually alert, but was less active because of age and, after 1830, illness. There was much truth in the complaint he made to his old friend Story about the "revolutionary spirit" on the Court.

It seemed certain that the Court, beleaguered outside and radically changed within, would have to modify its high nationalism to fit the new age. The question—and it was one on which the institutional future of the Court hung—was whether the modification would be a rout or an orderly retreat to solid nationalist ground. A sign of the change came, most appropriately, in the case of the *Steamboat Thomas Jefferson* (1825). To the surprise of the profession, Justice Story's opinion refused to extend the admiralty jurisdiction of the federal courts to the great system of inland lakes and rivers. The opinion was based on the doctrine of the common law that admiralty jurisdiction did not extend above the ebb and flow of the tide, but for Marshall (and perhaps others) the decisive factor was not the science of the law but the strategic vulnerability of the Court. Coming from the champion of federal admiralty jurisdiction at a time when the steamboat made a uniform admiralty law imperative on the inland waters, Story's decision prompted the *North American Review* (January, 1826), to remark, with some justification, that "high political sentiments and political emergencies" had brought the age of great judicial lawmaking temporarily to a close.

A more serious crisis of adjustment came, however, in interpreting the commerce clause. Here the retreat was decorous, if not entirely logical. To be sure, *Brown* v. *Maryland* (1827) revealed much of the old nationalist boldness and showed the Court's reluctance to abandon its high nationalism. But even here Marshall added a new note of judicial restraint by suggesting that "it might be premature to state any rule as being universal in its application" until the case demanded it. In *Willson* v. *Black Bird Creek Marsh Co.* two years later, Marshall substantially implemented the new spirit of restraint when he refused to void a Delaware law authorizing a bridge over a navigable stream that interfered with interstate commerce—though he clearly might have done so on the basis of precedent. As in the *Brown* case, the Court refused to draw a precise line between state and national commerce powers. But it did leave intact for later use its authority to do so and also preserved the nationalist principles of *Gibbons* v. *Ogden*.

Modifying its nationalism in contract cases was more painful for the Court—and more revealing of its inner tensions during this period of transition. In the *Sturges* opinion of 1819, when the Court struck down the New York bankruptcy act that applied to contracts made before the act, it touched only tangentially on the constitutionality of such a law when applied to subsequent contracts. This issue came before the Court in *Ogden* v. *Saunders* (1827), and it soon became apparent that the Court was bitterly divided—and had been divided even in 1819. Justice Johnson's majority opinion was appropriately Jeffersonian in rhetoric. He held that, in the absence of federal bankruptcy legislation, a state act which applied to contracts made after its passage was valid without qualification. Dismayed at this new tolerance for state regulation of property rights (though it was no more than the original meaning of the contract clause allowed), Marshall reiterated his *Sturges* position that under no circumstances could a state law obliterate the substance of a contract. For the first time in twenty-six years, he dissented from his colleagues on a major constitutional issue, and the company of Story and Duvall was little comfort.

"Ogden's case marks an epoch in our constitutional and judicial history," said the *United States Magazine and Democratic Review* later. "Painfully convinced that their constructive bow had been shot with vigor beyond the law, the Supreme Court, *de guerre lasse,* made a halt; and soon afterwards began retreat and atonement." *Providence Bank* v. *Billings* (1830) and several other cases of this period confirm the *United States Magazine*'s diagnosis. The question in the *Billings* case was whether a Rhode Island banking corporation was, by the implication of its charter, immune from a state tax on banking capital. Ignoring contrary precedents, which were pressed vigorously by counsel, Marshall affirmed the "vital importance" of the taxing power to the state and refused to diminish it. When Chief Justice Taney fell back on the *Billings* opinion seven years later to quash the doctrine of implied property rights, conservatives declared that ruling was no "legitimate principle of constitutional interpretation." But the language of the decision is very clear. The Court continued to moderate its use of the contract clause against state power in *Hawkins* v. *Barney's Lessee* (1831). Taking its cue from Kentucky states' rights opposition rather than its own decision in *Green* v. *Biddle,* the Court upheld the validity of occupying claimant laws. Marshall's final constitutional opinion two years later was another concession to state power. The question in *Barron* v. *Baltimore*

(1833) was whether the Fifth Amendment, and by extension the first ten amendments, restricted the states as well as the nation (a question that has plagued the modern Court). Marshall refused to countenance the idea. The amendments, he said, were intended to prevent the "general government" from encroaching on the essential liberties of the people and, unless explicitly stated, they could not be used to limit state power.

Perhaps Marshall sensed the irony of presenting an essay on limited government in his last constitutional opinion. If so, it probably reinforced his mounting conviction that the Court he knew was gone. Increasingly, the Court was doing just what John Taylor said it should do—make decisions, not law. But less and less were even decisions being made, for the Court had fallen progressively behind in its docket since the early 1830's. Moreover, because it was hampered by internal division, vacancies, and sickness, the Court could not resolve the great questions that came before it. *Worcester* v. *Georgia* (1832) was the one notable exception. Here the Chief Justice mobilized a majority and voided the laws of Georgia which violated the treaty between the Cherokee Indians and the United States. The Court had done its legal and moral duty, and conservative justices must have rejoiced that their decision was propaganda for the anti-Jackson campaign of 1832. But the decision was ignored by the state and left unenforced. The Indians, pondering no doubt the obscurity of the White Man's law, packed up for the brutal trek to the unhappy hunting grounds across the Mississippi. The Court's future seemed almost as bleak. As one democratic journal joyfully prophesied, "Goliah's [sic] sword, thus wrapped up, was put away in the temple, as we trust for a long rust."

Outside the courtroom, Marshall's carefully laid foundation of economic nationalism was being chipped away—politically by nullification, threats of secession, and Jacksonian states' rights; economically by Jackson's war on the Bank. With Congress and the Presidency radicalized and the Court "gone," Marshall sadly yielded, as he said, "to the conviction that our constitution cannot last." What had in fact happened—and Marshall can be forgiven for not appreciating it—was that the

Court, however unconsciously and reluctantly, saved itself by accommodating history.

The substance and method of this accommodation have led historians to tone down the image of a monolithic Court dominated by the Chief Justice, handing down impeccably certain law. Not only was division in the Court more frequent, it was now revealed outside the conference. Doctrinal compromise, especially on questions of state power, was the main theme of jurisprudence after 1825. The Court's friends in the legal profession and business community complained that these compromises broke too abruptly with established practice and, worse, left the meaning of the law uncertain. The extent to which the Taney Court was able to maneuver within that uncertainty (as Gerald Garvey perceptively observed in "The Constitutional Revolution of 1837 and the Myth of Marshall's Monolith," March, 1965) proves their point. Finally, examples of successful state resistance to the Court's decisions—outright opposition to *New Jersey* v. *Wilson, Green* v. *Biddle, Worcester* v. *Georgia,* as well as the legislative circumvention of *Dartmouth College* v. *Woodward*—show that excessive and categorical claims about the legal impact and institutional status of the Marshall Court are out of line.

Though the nationalist offensive of the Marshall Court was halted and much of its previous *esprit* and prestige had vanished, the pillars of Marshall's constitutional law remained. The nationalizing principles of the *Gibbons* opinion and the conservative ones of the *Yazoo* and *College* decisions were momentarily in disuse, but still available. The Bank was gone but not the doctrine of implied powers. And the Court's power to decide, though temporarily in abeyance, had not been permanently impaired. Whether the Court could or would preserve the principles and tradition of constitutional jurisprudence fashioned under Marshall—given the judicial division, the drift, and the mounting crisis of adjustment—was another question. The answer, and ironically history's appraisal of Chief Justice Marshall, rested squarely with the Jacksonian Court of Roger B. Taney. It was precisely this fact that worried the conservatives.

The old constitutional doctrines are fast fading away, and a change has come over the public mind, from which I augur little good.

JUSTICE JOSEPH STORY (1837)

FOUR

The Taney Court: Democracy Captures the Citadel

Unlike its illustrious predecessor, the Taney Court (1836–1864) was not an immediate favorite of history or historians. The *Dred Scott* decision of 1857 obliterated twenty-one years of effective judicial government and left the Court burdened with the moral obloquy of slavery, as well as a heavy share of war guilt. The Civil War itself—bringing freedom for the slaves and national consolidation—made the Taney Court not only appear un-American but historically irrelevant. The great multi-volume histories of the early postwar period—like those of Rhodes, Schouler, and Von Holst—hardly mention the Court, except for the shame of *Dred Scott* and the folly of judicial pretensions. Historiographical bias progressively diminished, however, as the passions of war subsided. In 1891, Hampton Carson (whose two-volume *Supreme Court of the United States* was one of the first general histories of the Court) concluded that the Taney Court had adjusted, not destroyed Marshall's constitutional system and that—slavery excepted—its accomplishments were "quite as essential to the full realization of our welfare as a nation" as those of "any preceding epoch in the history of the Court."

Subsequent scholars on the whole have agreed, but the implications of Carson's assessment were not apparent until the 1930's, when the Supreme Court abused its power and was unwilling to adjust the law to the crisis of depression. Since then, historians have approached the Taney period in a variety of ways: through judicial biography (Carl Swisher on Taney, Francis Weisenburger on Justice McLean, John P. Frank on Justice Daniel); through topical analysis (Felix Frankfurter on commerce and Benjamin Wright on contracts); and through general history (Charles Grove Haines and Foster H. Sherwood, *The Role of the Supreme Court in American Government and Politics 1835–1864* [1957], which is at present the only general account devoted entirely to the Taney period). But all concluded, implicitly if not explicitly, that the Taney Court's task was to bring the law into accord with the political and economic currents of the Age of Jackson, in other words, to preserve constitutional union by making it relevant to the new age. Unlike its predecessor, the Taney Court inherited a substantial body of decisional law. It had to adjust the old law, therefore, without appearing to abandon it—both for the sake of its own prestige and for the continued authority of the law; it had to balance continuity against change. And, the Court had to make this difficult adjustment while dealing with the disruption caused by new appointments and increased personal discord on the bench. The challenge was different from the one the Marshall Court had faced, but not less difficult. The accomplishment, most historians are inclined to concede, was scarcely less great.

The historical changes that brought the Jacksonians to power in 1828 and established a new frame of reference for the Taney Court amounted to a pervasive egalitarianism. Together the Enlightenment tradition of natural rights, revivalistic Protestantism, and abundant economic opportunity created a climate of militant individualism. The democratization of the political process reflected and, at the same time, supported the new intellectual and economic egalitarianism: universal white male suffrage was achieved by the mid-1820's and the direct election of electors by the 1830's; caucus nomination gave way to the national convention; and elective offices multiplied. As the national two-party system took shape in the 1830's, the twin principles of deference and gentleman rule, which had conditioned politics since the colonial period, disappeared. Government *by* as well as *for* the people seemed close to realization.

This new democratic America was also fully committed to the dream of inevitable economic progress. But conspicuously lacking was agreement on how to achieve progress, as well as any precise notion of what it meant. The most obvious change was that people no longer believed—as they had after the War of 1812—that the road to Utopia was a national mercantilism which would benefit all groups equally. The Panic of 1819 and the Missouri Debates of 1819–21 brought to light sectional differences which could not be served equitably by a single national plan. The admission of twelve new Western states during the Taney period further intensified the problem. State mercantilism seemed better equipped to accommodate the growing diversity. Paradoxically, at this time less economic nationalism rather than more seemed imperative to national union.

Whigs and Jacksonians alike were obliged to adjust to the new egalitarian spirit and to face the fact that unity on national economic policy, if it had ever existed, was gone. On the national level it was the party of Andrew Jackson that most quickly accommodated its organization, policy, and rhetoric to these new imperatives. The party organization—based on an intricate network of local, state, and national units, popular electioneering, and presidential patronage and prestige—was structured to exploit the potential of mass participatory democracy. Its economic policy, once it took shape, was a combination of egalitarian assumptions and the recognition that, in the face of self-conscious diversity, national economic planning would be fatal to political popularity and power. In short, the Jacksonian commitment to liberal economics was a negative one which abandoned national mercantilism. If government action were required, it was both democratic and practical to let the states take the initiative. This emphasis on state power, moreover, appealed to the state-based reform movement in the North, allowed the Southern states to do what they wanted with slavery, and, at the same time, permitted the Jacksonians to draw on the democratic capital of the Jeffersonian states' rights tradition. With Andrew Jackson as living proof that states' rights was not incompatible with national Union, the United States pushed on with the capitalist revolution, promising that its benefits would be equally dispersed and that the honesty and other simple virtues of the golden agrarian age would be preserved.

KING ANDREW'S COURT

To the immense discomfiture of conservatives, President Jackson was able to bring the Supreme Court into harmony with Jacksonian Democracy by virtue of seven appointments. Before Marshall's death in 1835, the President had already put three Democrats on the bench—John McLean (1829), Henry Baldwin (1830), and James Wayne (1835). Roger Taney's appointment to the Chief Justiceship in 1836, along with the appointments of Philip Barbour the same year and John Catron and John McKinley in 1837—to fill positions created by the judicial reorganization act of 1837—gave the Democrats an easy majority. Peter Daniel's last-minute appointment by Van Buren in 1841 left only Joseph Story and Smith Thompson representing the old Court.

Antebellum history seems to move by generations, and the Jacksonian judges clearly represented a new one. The differences were significant—and distasteful to many. The Whigs lamented the seven Democrats on the Court. The growing North distrusted the six judges from the South and West, as it later made only too plain, and felt itself underrepresented. The new justices lacked the common experience in the Revolution and the Confederation periods which had rallied the Marshall Court around nationalism. And, like the rest of the age, they were divided and contentious. Story regretted the radicalism and modest ability of some of his new brethren. Baldwin's sporadic madness and consistent paranoia and Daniel's chronic dissents impaired the efficiency of the Court, and McLean's perennial presidential aspirations detracted from its image. Opposition to Court Reporter Richard Peters (one of whose inadequacies was a handwriting that not even he could read) and the struggle over his removal in 1843 turned latent dissension on the Court into outright factionalism. But even before that, Court unity had disintegrated.

It was seeing Roger Taney in John Marshall's chair, however, that chilled the spirits of the old Court's friends more than anything else. Chief Justice Marshall had become synonymous with the Court and, after him, none could please. Story, who would have come closest, wanted the Chief Justiceship badly but he had to resign himself to being passed over by his omnipotent political enemies. But the conservative mind veritably boggled at the prospect of Taney, that "supple, cringing tool of power," Taney, the advocate of states' rights, a co-author of the Veto Message which condemned the Second Bank of the United States, and the Secretary of the Treasury that executed the sentence. Stooped, sallow, ugly, and a Catholic too. By no stretch of generosity could critics make Taney fit the Marshall mold.

The prophets of gloom were correct in predicting change but were badly mistaken in assuming that a changed Court was no Court at all. Less paranoic contemporaries saw much ground for hope, and history soon confirmed their optimism. Whatever their previous political habits and whatever the reasons for their appointment, the new justices were nobody's minions—once they donned the ermine. Common social and professional connections with the business community and dedication to the sanctity of property cut across sectional and intellectual differences. Respect for the law, devotion to the Court, and a sense of duty to the nation provided a common working ground.

Not the least of the new Court's assets, as Carl Swisher's distinguished biography shows, was its Chief Justice. Roger Taney suited the complex and contradictory middle period of American history as much as any man could. He was a Southerner who loved his country, a states' righter dedicated to the Union, a slaveholder who regretted the institution and manumitted his slaves, and an aristocrat with a democratic political philosophy. In Maryland he had practiced law and politics simultaneously and succeeded in both. After abandoning Federalism as a losing cause, he rose to the top of the state's Jacksonian machine. As United States Attorney General (1831–33) and Secretary of the Treasury (1833), he revealed an anti-monopolistic, state mercantilist, democratic bias that made him one of President Jackson's closest advisers. He brought this bias to the Chief Justiceship, along with a high intelligence and legal acumen, kindness and humility, patriotism, and a determination to be a great Chief Justice that enabled him to mold the modest raw materials of the Court into an effective and prestigious institution. To be sure, it was not the Marshall Court. But, then again, it was not the age of Marshall.

CORPORATIONS AND THE COURT: THE NEW LOOK

The Chief Justice made his debut wearing long trousers instead of the small clothes of the Marshall period, a sartorial omen that a new age had begun—a sure portent, one journal remarked grimly, of a "modern sans-culotte-ism." * The three great constitutional cases of the 1837 term confirmed conservative fears. Each had been argued before the Marshall Court, but, because of divisions and absences, none had been determined. In each of these decisions, the new Court modified a doctrine of the "old law"; together, the decisions presented a rough outline of the democratic posture Taney's Court would assume in the new age.

Of these three cases, the *Charles River Bridge* v. *Warren Bridge* (1837) was the first, the most dramatic and revealing. The facts raised crucial and delicate issues. In 1785, the Massachusetts legislature had chartered the Charles River Bridge Company to build a bridge across the Charles River connecting Boston and Cambridge and had granted the company the right to collect tolls for forty years, a privilege later extended to seventy years. In 1828, while the toll rights of this company were still in force, the legislature chartered the Warren Bridge Company, giving it authority to build an adjacent toll-free bridge. The question was this: Did the imprecise wording of the old charter implicitly confer a monopoly on the Charles River Bridge Company which the new bridge encroached upon, thus violating the contract clause of the Constitution and the *Dartmouth College* ruling?

On this technical legal question hinged major political, economic, and intellectual issues of the age, issues which sharply divided the Whigs from the Jacksonians. Warren Dutton, speaking for the Charles River Bridge Company and for the Whigs, reminded the Court that an adverse decision would extinguish half a million dollars in property outright and jeopardize another ten million. Gone, too, he predicted, would be public faith in the government's promises and, with that, the venture capital so critical to corporate development. On the other hand, the claims of the new bridge were important to the

---

* *Small clothes* was the term for the style worn in the early republic—snug pants fitting tightly below the knee. *Sans-culotte* ("without such pants") was a term used during the French Revolution, which literally referred to those who wore trousers, but symbolically, to those who were democrats and radicals.

legislature if it was to serve public needs produced by new circumstances and not be hamstrung by acts of its predecessors. As for private property and economic progress, it was insisted that the old bridge had already paid for itself several times over. Besides, asked counsel for the new bridge company, how could new modes of transportation like the railroad be developed if every dilapidated turnpike and canal company could entrench itself behind an implied monopoly?

The Chief Justice spoke for the majority in an opinion that disconcerted his critics by its persuasiveness ("smooth and plausible," admitted Webster, who was counsel for the Charles River Bridge Company, "but cunning and jesuitical"). Against the doctrine of implied contracts, Taney mobilized Anglo-American law and Jacksonian politics and economics. It was a rule of common law, he declared, known in every case "without exception" and supported by fifty years of American "usage and practice," that "any ambiguity in the terms of the contract, must operate against the adventurers, and in favor of the public." "While the rights of private property are sacredly guarded," Taney continued in good Jacksonian style, "we must not forget that the community also have rights, and that the happiness and well-being of every citizen depends on their faithful preservation." In addition, both equality of opportunity and economic progress militate against implied monopoly. If every turnpike and canal company could take refuge behind implied monopoly, said Taney, following the lead of counsel, then "modern science" would be throttled and transportation set back to the last century. Neither economic progress nor the state's power to serve the public good could be interdicted on the shaky grounds of legal inference and construction. The charter of the new bridge was constitutional.

Justice Story liked public welfare and economic progress as much as the Chief Justice, but believing them inseparable from the absolute security of private property, he dissented bitterly from the "speculative niceties and novelties" of his new brethren. His point-by-point refutation of Taney convinced only his old colleague Justice Thompson on the Court. Across the land, however, conservatives read his scholarly disquisition as Marshallian orthodoxy—and they were right. But mistakenly, they concluded a revolution had occurred in American law.

The Court had, in fact, neither opposed the corporation per se nor departed from the *Dartmouth College* ruling that a corporate charter was a contract protected by the contract clause of the Constitution. Had the rights claimed by the Charles River Bridge Company been explicitly granted, there is little doubt that the Court would have upheld them. The real significance of the *Bridge* decision was the Court's refusal to extend by implication the rule of the *Dartmouth College* case— a rule both Marshall and Story would have extended. Two assumptions were behind this refusal: First, the Court recognized that the new corporate device combining economic privilege and political power posed a danger to the public welfare, especially when select economic interests were given monopolistic powers by special legislative charter. Second, the Court admitted it should restrain itself whenever possible from challenging the representatives of the people when they act to protect that welfare. Above all, and Taney made this explicit, the Court should not venture into the legal no man's land of inference to nullify legislation passed to protect the public good.

It should not be assumed from the *Bridge* decision that the Supreme Court dominated the field of corporate regulation, for in fact most regulations were made on the state level. The legislative charter specifying limitations on the corporate operation was the primary means of regulation. And the interpretation of such grants took place largely in the state courts. (As it turned out, the problem of effective control was less a legal one of judicial construction than a political one of getting meaningful regulations through state legislatures that were pressured by powerful lobbies and burdened by incompetence.) In other, more direct ways, state judiciaries entered the regulatory field. Writs of mandamus and quo warranto—the former designed to compel the performance of duties stipulated in the charter and the latter to obtain a forfeiture of the charter in case of nonperformance—were devices available in the state courts for use against corporations. As early as 1807, state courts acted to protect the public from corporate abuses by holding that corporations were suable in tort, that is, for private or civil wrongs committed independent of contract.

However, the Supreme Court did touch various phases of this regulatory process at vital points. And under Taney its actions were guided by the spirit of economic realism and judicial self-restraint that were apparent in the *Bridge* decision. The interpretation of corporate charters was a case in point. Charters, especially those extending unusual privileges—such as the monopoly granted to a railroad corporation in *Richmond F. & P.R.R.* v. *Louisa R.R.* (1851)—were constructed narrowly and viewed by the Taney Court with an eye to the public welfare. In *Ohio Life Insurance & Trust* v. *Debolt* (1854), the Court conceded the constitutionality of a charter grant of tax exemption but refused to extend such a privilege by implication. Taney made clear that its refusal was based on a recognition of some unpleasant realities in business life. Bills of incorporation, he noted, were almost always drawn up by the parties "personally interested" in getting concessions rather than by impartial representatives of the public. Moreover, such bills "are often passed by the Legislature in the last days of its session when, from the nature of our political institutions, the business is unavoidably transacted in a hurried manner, and it is impossible that every member can deliberately examine every provision in every bill upon which he is called on to act." In addition to this strict construction of corporate charters, the Court also endorsed the use of mandamus, quo warranto, and tort law by state courts against unauthorized corporate power. And in *West River Bridge Co.* v. *Dix* (1848), the Court sanctioned the doctrine of eminent domain, permitting state legislatures to take corporate property for public uses with just compensation. This rule, boasted the democratic Boston *Post,* heralded a "new era" of popular rights over corporate monopoly.

If there were some areas of corporate development in which the Court played a supporting role, there were others, such as interstate expansion of corporate business, where it took the lead. In *Bank of Augusta* v. *Earle* (1839), agents of three out-of-state banking corporations purchased bills of exchange (the primary source of interstate commercial credit at this time) in Alabama. But the men who had issued these bills cynically refused to honor them on the grounds that foreign banking corporations were not permitted to operate in Alabama. Justice McKinley heard the case on circuit, and, as Justice Story recalled, "frightened half the lawyers and all the corporations of the country out of their properties," by upholding the defaulters. Had the Supreme Court affirmed McKinley's opinion, it would have dealt a mortal blow to the interstate operation of corporations.

The Jacksonians were still rejoicing and the Whigs lamenting, when the Court reversed McKinley's sweeping interdict. Taney tactfully applied the doctrine of comity, holding that if a corporation founded in one state was authorized by charter to do business in another, it could do so unless specifically prohibited by the law of the other state. Silence would be interpreted to mean that the state had no objection to foreign corporations doing business within its boundaries. Taney found nothing to undo this presumption in the Alabama case.

Compared to the radical democracy of McKinley's circuit opinion, the Taney decision seemed—and was so labelled by democratic purists—a sellout to the corporation. In fact, it was an expedient concession to the realities of American economic life that was generally consistent with the Court's Jacksonian posture. The decision armed the state with great potential power. Moreover, the Court had resisted Webster's argument that the corporation was a citizen with all the constitutional rights and privileges thereof (although there was material at hand for such an interpretation had the Court been inclined to use it). Taney's opinion, together with Justice Thompson's circuit decision in the *Warren Manufacturing Co.* v. *Aetna Insurance Co.* (1837)—upholding a law making a Connecticut corporation doing business in Maryland suable in the latter's courts and making judgments brought in such cases suable in federal courts—showed that the Court had no intention of leaving the state at the mercy of interstate corporations. If the states did little to control these corporations, it was not because of the hostility of the Taney Court.

Briscoe v. *Commonwealth Bank of Kentucky,* the second of the three famous cases of the 1837 term, concerned state banking. Of all the corporate issues of the period, banking was the most comprehensive and the most likely to bring the Court under political and economic attack. This was because both state and nation were active in the area and had assumed competing roles. It was only natural, therefore, that during the 1830's banking should come to serve as the battleground in the contest between state and national mercantilism. Moreover, as credit and currency manipulation were alien to the mentality of the small farmer, banking became a focal point in the debate over honest labor and the good life which divided the agrarian- and commercial-minded. Not surprisingly, both Jacksonian policy and Jacksonian rhetoric were shaped in the war against the "parasitic" "monied aristocracy" of the Second Bank of the United States. But as champions of economic progress, the Jacksonians could not afford to be against all banks. In supporting state banking, they deferred to economic realities, they broadened economic opportunity, and they also indulged their preference for state over national mercantilism.

The Commonwealth Bank of Kentucky fit into the Jacksonian economic plan. Though nominally a private corporation, the bank's stock was owned solely by the state, its president and board of directors were chosen by the legislature, and its notes circulated as money. The crucial issue was whether these notes were bills of credit prohibited by Article I, Section 10 of the Constitution. John Marshall's answer was well known to the Court. In the parallel case of *Craig* v. *Missouri* (1830), he had—speaking for the majority—declared against state issuance of paper money. And when the Kentucky case was argued in 1834, Marshall was prepared to bring it within the scope of the *Craig* ruling.

In 1837, however, circumstances were different. President Jackson had made good his promise: Nicholas Biddle's Bank was dead. And, by default, state banks now constituted the main source of national currency and credit. Justice McLean, in the majority opinion, accommodated both this blunt economic fact and Jacksonian principles by holding that the notes of the Commonwealth Bank of Kentucky were not bills of credit interdicted by the Constitution, even though the state owned the bank and the notes circulated by state law as legal tender. McLean went through the motions of distinguishing the *Kentucky* from the *Craig* case. But it was obvious to all that technical law had given way to economic and political expediency. As McLean admitted, an opinion against the Kentucky bank would be "a fatal blow against the state banks, which have a capital of near $400,000,000, and which supply almost the entire circulating medium of the country." Justice Story stood on the *Craig* decision and in a bitter, solitary dissent condemned the new spirit of expediency which had set the Court "adrift from its former moorings." Delivered with "profound reverence and affection" for John Marshall, Story's dissent marked the distance the new Court had strayed from the path of the "old law."

THE TANEY COURT AND THE COMMERCE CLAUSE

Thanks in large part to Marshall, the commerce clause was the most effective constitutional instrument the Court had for allocating power between the states and the nation. And it was inevitable, with the American tendency to view fundamental economic and political problems in terms of state versus nation, that the commerce clause should become the center of debate. Some adjustments in the clause were clearly in order. (A complete discussion of this can be found in Frankfurter's previously mentioned *The Commerce Clause under Marshall, Taney, and Waite*.) The Marshall Court had painted with broad strokes. The new age needed a lighter touch and more subtle shading. National prosperity based on expansive national commerce was desired no less than before. But neither Southern nor Northern states would tolerate commerce interpretations that encroached on their prerogatives—the former because of slavery and the latter because of an interest in reform legislation (including anti-slavery laws). A delicate interpretation of the commerce power was needed, one which would please both North and South and, at the same time, would encourage national commerce. This was the acid test for judicial statesmanship.

New York v. Miln (1837) brought the Court face to face with the problem. New York had passed a law in 1824 that required masters of all vessels arriving at the Port of New York from foreign countries or from other states to report the names, ages, occupations, and other data of all passengers and to take bond that none should become wards of the city. This law was designed to keep the city from being overwhelmed with indigents it was not prepared to care for. The state argued that such legislation fell within its authority to protect the health and welfare of its citizens. But the law seemed clearly to touch interstate commerce, and the question raised was whether it was an unconstitutional encroachment of Congress' power over that area.

The Court might have closed the door to state power by opening the one to exclusivism deliberately left ajar by Marshall's Gibbons opinion. And it was pressured to do so by Story's assurance that Marshall would have wanted that. However, Justice Barbour's opinion for the majority followed Jacksonian priorities, rather than those espoused by Marshall. The New York regulation, said Barbour, was a valid exercise of police power, which he defined vaguely as state authority to legislate for the safety, happiness, and general welfare of the people within its jurisdiction. He cited Marshall's tangential references to police power in the Gibbons and Brown opinions as his authorities. But Barbour's contention that police power was "unqualified and exclusive" went far beyond anything that precedent or practice could justify. He erroneously assumed that police regulations could be entirely separated from interstate commerce, flatly contradicted the Gibbons opinion which gave federal law priority in case of conflict, and ignored both the Tenth Amendment to the Constitution and Article VI by establishing just by definition and assertion an area of state power which was prior to, outside the scope of, and superior to that power delegated to Congress. Story saw the oversimplifications, was appalled at their radical import, and dissented forcefully on the basis of *Gibbons* v. *Ogden*.

The *Miln* opinion settled nothing except that the New York regulation was not unconstitutional. The Court remained bitterly divided over the basic questions of whether congressional power over interstate commerce was exclusive or concurrent with the states, and whether it extended to slaves. The amorphous concept of police power (not even its advocates could define it) was at best an expedient means of avoiding open division on the Court; but, as rendered by Justice Barbour, it was not even that. When Barbour delivered his opinion on the last day of the term, several of his colleagues were shocked to discover that the opinion's assertions about the scope of police power went beyond the position accepted in conference and did not have the concurrence of a majority.

Confusion and uncertainty about the meaning of the commerce clause continued in the *License Cases* (1847) and the *Passenger Cases* (1849). Both raised the question of whether state welfare and reform legislation affecting interstate commerce was an unconstitutional encroachment on congressional power. At issue in the *License Cases* were the temperance laws of Massachusetts, Rhode Island, and New Hampshire. In the first two states, the law required state licenses for retailers of imported liquor in less than bulk quantity; in the latter the statute required a license whether the liquor was sold wholesale or retail, without distinction as to quantity.

Again the Court was able to decide the case but not the law. Nine justices agreed that the laws were valid but were unable to agree in nine separate opinions by six judges—none of which had the support of a majority—on their reasons for thinking so. Taney's opinion upheld the Massachusetts and Rhode Island laws by Marshall's "just and safe" *Brown* ruling, which permitted states to tax imports once the "original package" had been broken. The New Hampshire law was a different matter, since it licensed bulk as well as retail sales. In upholding this law, Taney explicitly repudiated exclusivism and supported the power of states to legislate concurrently with

Congress in the field of interstate commerce, though he made it clear that in case of a conflict between state and national laws, the latter were "superior and controlling." He went out of his way to play down the police power concept, which he thought extraneous and "nothing more or less than the powers of government inherent in every sovereignty to the extent of its dominions."

With a convenient suspension of logic, Justice McLean refuted Marshall's original package rule: he insisted on the exclusive power of Congress but then avoided the impractical consequences by supporting an extreme version of police power. Peter Daniel rejected the involved reasoning of his colleagues, the "glosses of essay-writers, lecturers, and commentators" and substituted instead the proposition that states controlled all the property within their jurisdictions, regardless of derivation. He went on, as Barbour had ten years earlier, to reverse the whole concept of reserved powers by declaring: "Every power delegated to the Federal government must be expounded in coincidence with a perfect right in the States to all that they have not delegated. . . ." Justice Woodbury paid respects to Daniel's extreme position as well as the concurrent power concept, but he subscribed to the Jacksonian proviso that doubtful cases be resolved in favor of the states. John Catron relied on concurrent power, Robert Grier on police—though he was not bold enough to say what it meant. Justice Nelson sided with Catron and Taney. Altogether the Court agreed on nothing and left its law without a reasoned justification.

The *Passenger Cases* two years later climaxed the Court's doctrinal and personal disunity over commerce and brought it into the open. At issue were the laws of Massachusetts and New York which taxed immigrants coming into the ports of the state. Massachusetts, once the seat of constitutional nationalism, was now sharply divided between those advocating national commerce through national power and those who wanted sufficient state power to keep out undesirable aliens and to tax for the public welfare. The rising forces of anti-slavery were among the champions of state power; they saw it as a weapon against the fugitive slave law. (Daniel Webster was embarrassed by the schism and berated his state for its "ultraism, mock-morals, false philanthropy and illiberal laws infringing trade and commercial intercourse.") To add to the confusion, the Southern states violently objected to the North's use of police power and states' rights against slavery, but they were obliged to support the doctrines themselves to defend their own laws against the immigration of free Negroes.

The Court's decision reflected these contradictory desires and made no constitutional sense. After three arguments, the Court came up with eight separate and discursive opinions running to nearly two hundred pages. A precarious majority of five struck down the laws as conflicting with federal law but continued to disagree on their reasons. Despite Justice Wayne's attempt to reduce the majority position to order, the Court reporter had to conclude that there was no opinion of the Court.

Not only were the judges unable to agree, but they foolishly aired their previous disagreement over the *Miln* case. Wayne took particular care to diminish the authority of that decision by noting that Barbour's last-minute discourse on the commerce clause (printed in the *Reports* with the apparent sanction of the Chief Justice) went beyond the decision of the conference and was concurred in by only two justices. Taney, seconded by Daniel, answered Wayne's charges, reminding him that if the authority of the opinions could be undone by one justice's "individual memory," the "public confidence" in the Court was done for. That confidence had already been shaken to the extent that neither lawyers nor statesmen knew where the Court had been or where it was going.

Not until *Cooley* v. *Board of Wardens* (1852) did the Court inject some constitutional order into its interpretation of the commerce power. The case provided an ideal opportunity. In 1803, Pennsylvania had passed a pilotage law for the Port of Philadelphia which required ships entering or leaving the port to take on pilots or pay half the pilotage fee into a fund for the relief of distressed pilots. Since pilotage was obviously connected with navigation and thus with commerce, the Pennsylvania law raised a clear question of state power to regulate commerce. Congress had twice legislated on pilotage but in neither case was there any conflict with the Pennsylvania law. The issue came, therefore, precisely and unavoidably to focus on exclusive versus concurrent power—whether the constitutional grant of commerce power to Congress automatically prohibited state regulation of commerce or whether states could regulate commerce as long as such regulations did not actually conflict with congressional legislation. This was the fundamental issue on which the Court had been divided since 1837, if not 1824.

Justice Benjamin R. Curtis, who replaced Woodbury in 1851, helped break the deadlock. He had no strikingly original ideas on the problem and in fact drew liberally on his predecessor's opinion in the *License Cases* as well as on Webster's *Gibbons* argument. But he did have a sharp mind and a lucid pen, and, since he was not identified with either side, he was able to provide the neutral ground for a compromise. His clear and refreshingly short opinion started from the undeniable proposition that the commerce power granted Congress did not expressly exclude the states from exercising authority over matters of interstate commerce. Exclusive congressional jurisdiction in an area, he went on, could only come when the subject matter itself made it imperative. But the subject of commerce was vast and various and did not require exclusivism. Some matters, he said, needed a "single uniform rule, operating equally on the commerce of the United States in every port." Some just as certainly required diversity. Curtis then expounded a rule to cover the complex nature of commerce: Power follows necessity. If the matter in question requires uniformity, then the power belongs to Congress; if diversity, it belongs to the states. The regulation of pilots in the port of Philadelphia, he concluded, falls in the latter category, so the Pennsylvania law is constitutional.

McLean and Wayne, whom Curtis called the "most high-toned Federalists on the bench," dissented. Taking up Story's role as the preacher of gloom, McLean prophesied that the retreat from nationalism would return the republic to the chaos of the confederation period. Justice Daniel concurred in the majority verdict but not in its reasoning and defended state action with his doctrine of "original and inherent" state power.

"Selective exclusiveness," as the Court's approach came to be called, was not a certain and final answer to the problem of allocating the commerce power between state and nation—as subsequent attempts to apply the rule revealed. Curtis gave no clues beyond the case as to which aspects of commerce required uniformity, which diversity. Nor did he supply any specific criteria for determining these essential categories. In fact, the significant feature of the decision was not the formulation of a definitive doctrine but the Court's tacit agreement to stop looking for one, as well as its decision to operate case-by-case on the basis of practicality, common sense, and economic realism. This new spirit was evident not only in the repudiation of exclusivism and the undogmatic solution of "selective exclusiveness" but in the Court's reasoning in the case. The opinion was ten pages long, was deliberately limited to the case at hand, made no reference to precedent (not even to *Gibbons* and *Brown*), and was guided by the principle that the rule of law should conform to the facts of life. By insisting on rigid doctrine and objecting to the majority's pragmatic definition of power, McLean and Daniel merely highlighted the new pragmatism.

In retreating from constitutional formalism, the Court willed to do what it had previously done unwillingly: it decided cases without a definitive pronouncement of doctrine. The important difference now was that the Court devised a rule of thumb to guide the process of decision and thus gave clarity and some predictability to its efforts as well as confidence to the profession and the nation.

Choosing process over doctrine enabled the Taney Court to restrain its power without surrendering it—and judicial restraint was the order of the day. The Marshall Court, especially after 1825, sensed this and acted accordingly, but with reluctance. The new generation of judges responded more willingly and more openly. Assumptions, deriving from Marshall, that the states were axiomatically untrustworthy and the Court was the guardian appointed to save the people from their legislative impulses gave way to a more modest version of the Court's role.

Chief Justice Taney's first constitutional opinion sounded this theme of the new jurisprudence, and his colleagues—Daniel in the *License Cases,* Wayne in the *Passenger Cases,* and Woodbury in *United States* v. *New Bedford Bridge* (1847) to mention a few—followed. The Court "acting on its own views of what justice required," declared the Chief Justice in his *Bridge* opinion, should not raise up an implied contract, "by a sort of judicial coercion," where the legislature had chosen not to do so. In the Dorr Rebellion case of *Luther* v. *Borden* (1849), the Court was more precise about what it should not do. "Political questions," Taney said, belong to the political branches and are beyond the competence of the judicial process. And the rival governments' conflicting claims to legality in Rhode Island (as well as the issue of domestic violence) fell within that nonjudicial category. While the Court "should always be ready to meet any question confided to it by the Constitution, it is equally its duty not to pass beyond its appropriate sphere of action." And even in spheres less clearly "political," the Chief Justice advised caution. When the majority attempted to judge the competing claims of railroads and steamboats in *Pennsylvania* v. *Wheeling and Belmont Bridge Co.* (1851), Taney and Daniel sharply dissented. Without legislative guidelines from Congress, argued Taney, the Court should not substitute its discretion for that of the state, for there are—because of the "narrow scope of judicial proceedings"—many duties which the Court "is utterly incapable of discharging." Six years later in *Dred Scott* v. *Sanford,* Taney and his associates proved the validity of that simple truth by forgetting it.

CONTINUITY VERSUS CHANGE: THE HAUNTING PRESENCE OF JOHN MARSHALL

When the conservatives took stock at the end of the 1837 term, they found "the whole fair system of the Constitution beginning to dissolve like the baseless fabric of a vision." Yet, ten years later Justice Wayne, a Jacksonian, felt compelled to praise the Marshall period as an age of "giants" and to rejoice that "the structure raised by them for the defense of the constitution, has not this day been weakened by their successors." Henry Clay agreed that the "structure" was still intact and revised his previous condemnation of Taney to read: "No man in the United States could have been selected, more abundantly able to wear the ermine which Chief Justice Marshall honored." What obviously had *not* occurred was the constitutional upheaval prophesied by Story, Kent, and Webster. The Court's firm commitments to economic progress and corporate capitalism, as well as the legal and moral premises underlying it, still remained.

Considering the American greed for land, the legacy of the Marshall Court, and the Southern and Western complexion of the Taney Court, it is not surprising that agrarian capitalism continued to have high priority. The Taney Court did resist some of the most exorbitant demands of the speculator and occasionally a dissenting justice (Daniel, for example, in *Arguello* v. *United States,* 1855) spoke for the little man. But the majority of the Court permitted land speculators to acquire hundreds of thousands of acres of public domain against the advice of the government and the interest of the settlers. And the Court further assisted agrarian capitalism by opening these new lands to the Southern slavery system.

However, the *Charles River Bridge* decision made it perfectly clear that the Court's interest in capitalism was not limited to the agrarian kind. The opposition to charter rights by implication in that decision stemmed not from hostility but solicitude toward commercial expansion and corporate enterprise. The disagreement in the Court was over means: Story, speaking for the old Court, argued that absolute contractual sanctity was essential for capital investment; Taney insisted that monopoly, by inference, would deter rather than advance investment. Even the change in means was moderate, for the pro-corporate law of the *Dartmouth College* decision was left in force. To be sure, a number of "sound lawyers" (like Daniel Webster) and businessmen of established wealth (like Harrison Gray Otis) never learned to live with Taney's opinion. But the new wave of entrepreneurs and their professional allies, along with some of the old guard (like the counsel for the new bridge company Simon Greenleaf, or Charles Sumner, or Court Reporter Richard Peters), saw it as an encouragement to corporate development. The phenomenal growth of the corporation in the thirty years following the *Bridge* decision proved them correct; it also proved that the Taney Court was a friend of property and commerce.

The Court's firm attachment to the sanctity of private property was even clearer in subsequent contract cases involving the state debtor relief laws that grew out of the depression of 1837. In four cases, such laws were struck down as violations of the contract clause, though in one (*Bronson* v. *Kinzie,* 1843) Taney reaffirmed the state's right to regulate contractual remedies (the means of enforcing the contract) and the right to impose regulations on subsequent contracts. In *Rowan et al.* v. *Runnels* (1847), the Court made it clear that state courts had no more right to void contracts than state legislatures.

Even in cases which pitted state need to tax against corporate exemption privileges, the Court continued to support property. The opinion in *Gordon* v. *Appeal Tax Court* (1845) used Marshall's extremely conservative ruling in *New Jersey* v. *Wilson* as precedent to uphold a general state law granting tax exemptions to state banks. *Piqua Branch of the State Bank of Ohio* v. *Knoop* (1853) carried on this line. That case raised the question of whether a state legislature could surrender its sovereignty to the extent of granting perpetual corporate tax exemptions. Against bitter state opposition and the dissent of Taney and three other justices, the Court upheld such a grant and declared it came under the contract clause of the Constitution. When the Ohio Constitutional Convention countered by passing an amendment repealing such tax exemptions, the Court struck it down in *Dodge* v. *Woolsey* (1855) as a violation of the contract clause. Chief Justice Taney, who did not view state banks with the same suspicion as other corporations, went with the majority. But the Southern agrarians—Catron, Daniel, and Campbell—dissented, charging that the corporation was turning the republic into a Turkish Empire with the Court's assistance. Many democrats across the country wondered if they weren't right.

If the Court was helpful to corporate capitalism on the state level, on the national level it was indispensable to its expansion. As previously noted, *Bank of Augusta* v. *Earle* (1839) conceded the right of corporations chartered in one state to do business in others. Though states might prohibit such intrusions, the rule that silence implied consent unleashed nationalizing forces of commerce which were to alter the very nature of federalism. As the New York *Courier* put it, Taney's opinion was "as far from Loco-Foco doctrine as Alexander Hamilton himself could have desired."

One favor called for another. Corporations like those in the *Bank of Augusta* case—chartered in one state but doing business in another—feared discrimination in the courts of the second state and insisted on jurisdictional access to the more impartial, hopefully pro-business, federal courts. Marshall's opinion in *Bank of the United States* v. *Deveaux* (1809), which had brought corporations under the diversity of citizenship jurisdiction, seemed at first to cover the situation. But subsequent rulings that cases under diversity jurisdiction would be barred if any stockholder of the corporation was a citizen of the same state as that of the opposing party took back most of what had been given, especially with the increasingly broad base of stock ownership. The Taney Court came to the rescue of corporations which wanted access to federal courts, thereby eliminating a "great anomaly in our jurisprudence," as Story put it. In *Louisville Railroad* v. *Letson* (1844), the Court held that, for jurisdictional purposes, the corporation would be presumed to be a citizen of the state in which it had been chartered. The constant increase in the corporate business of the federal courts suggests that corporate interests realized some of the anticipated advantages. There was no doubt that federal jurisdiction contributed to the formation of a uniform body of law which was indispensable to the business community's national expansion.

Swift v. *Tyson* (1842) represented a further effort by the Court to facilitate national commerce through uniform commercial law. This case was an action on a bill of exchange, which came before the Court on diversity of citizenship jurisdiction. It had been understood that, in cases involving diversity jurisdiction, the Court was bound by Section 34 of the Judiciary Act of 1789 to render decisions according to the state laws which applied—in *Swift* v. *Tyson,* those of New York. On the point at issue here, however, there was no controlling statute and New York courts had established no conclusive rule. Justice Story took this opportunity (as Charles Warren's "New Light on the History of the Federal Judiciary Act of 1789" [1923] shows) to change the intended meaning of Section 34. He held that "laws" in Section 34 did not include state court decisions and that, in the absence of a controlling statute, federal courts were free to apply general principles of commercial law. But because of the state's refusal to withdraw from the field and the inability of federal judges to agree on what the "general law" of commerce was, Story's opinion produced chaos instead of uniformity. Until it was declared unconstitutional in 1938, the decision invited federal courts to usurp state judicial and legislative authority in the areas of contracts, agency, insurance, and damages.

Much more successful was Chief Justice Taney's own effort on behalf of uniform commercial law in *The Genesee Chief* v. *Fitzhugh* (1851). The Marshall Court had ruled (*Steamboat Thomas Jefferson,* 1825) that the admiralty and maritime jurisdiction of the federal courts did not extend to rivers and other inland bodies of water, except where the tide ebbed and flowed. The effect of the decision was to turn over to state courts and legislatures the job of making legal order out of the rising volume of steamboat commerce on the great inland system of navigable lakes and rivers—and, in consequence, there was no order. In an explicitly pragmatic response to commercial necessity, Taney reversed Story's earlier ruling, declaring it founded in mistaken law and bad policy, and extended the admiralty jurisdiction of federal courts over the whole system of inland waterways. Marshall, who never liked the *Jefferson* decision, would surely have congratulated his successor.

THE CASE FOR JUDICIAL STATESMANSHIP

The Taney Court discourages easy evaluation. Its preference for expediency over doctrine, the resulting uneven mixture of change and continuity, its unheroic style—all obscure the direction of the Court's jurisprudence and provide few great moments to celebrate. Whether or not for this reason, scholars have been slow about exploring the Taney period. Though there is considerable room for refinement, this much is clear: before the Court was drawn into the vortex of the slavery controversy, it shaped constitutional law to serve the political and economic imperatives of the new age. Moreover, it did this in such a way as to make a permanent contribution to the structure of American jurisprudence.

In short, the Court's claim to statesmanship is that it chose what to preserve and what to change with discrimination and historical discernment. Among the historical constants which the Taney Court recognized and used as the foundation for its law were the basic cultural premises of American capitalism. Commercial law—contracts, agency, bills and notes, insurance, tort—continued to rest on the nineteenth-century assumption that man was rational enough to know what he was doing and moral enough to accept responsibility for what he did. The Court showed no doubt, either, that economic enterprise and social progress went hand-in-hand, and it acted on the corollary assumption that the law served the latter by encouraging the former. In this spirit the Court under Taney gave legal form to the rising business corporation and made a place for it— consistent with the Marshall Court's early efforts—in the emerging intellectual system of individual free enterprise. Commercial nationalism also continued to be a part of judicial policy. And the Court managed to surmount states' rights barriers in both the North and South and establish a viable constitutional basis for interstate commerce. Finally, modified though it was, the contract clause remained the constitutional shield for private property.

Not only did the Court carry on the capitalist-oriented law of the Marshall Court, but it did so while introducing changes suitable to Jacksonian democracy. As national mercantilism declined and the business corporation rose, the Court, following Jacksonian priorities, modified constitutional federalism to accommodate the new responsibilities which fell to the states in banking, internal improvements, and economic promotion and regulation. Basic to the constitutional position of the Marshall Court was the assumption that the complementary goals of economic and political nationalism depended on expanding congressional power to promote interstate capitalism (as in the American Plan) and restricting state power so it could not interfere with it. The Marshall Court knew from experience that Congress did not intend to use this power to *regulate* commerce; it had already imposed safe limits on the state power to do so. The implication was clear: the legal guidelines for the new economic age should come through judicial decisions, not the statutory mandates of faction-ridden, popularly controlled state legislatures.

Facing the realities of corporate power which the Marshall Court had ignored, the Taney Court not only recognized the state as a promotional agency but a regulatory one as well. This dual concept of state power should serve as a warning against concluding, as some scholars have done, that Jacksonian democracy was synonymous with economic laissez faire. The Taney Court was able to adjust because it rejected the earlier Court's assumption that state power was inherently hostile to the public interest and fatal to the Union. Since it was free from anti-democratic, anti-state prejudices, the Court under Taney could grasp the central fact of early nineteenth-century government: the states, as Jacksonian Justice Levi Woodbury put it, were the "great fountains of legislation" and the vital source of experimentation in both policy and administration. Above all, the Court understood and acted on the theory—the same on which Jacksonian political and economic policy was predicated—that the states, not the nation, were best able to handle the diverse and conflicting economic demands of a sectionally divided nation. Viewing the states in a new historical light, the Court devised a fresh approach to state power. As Justice Woodbury put it in *Planter's Bank* v. *Sharp et al.* (1848), the states, when acting "in matters of general interest," "must be presumed to act from public considerations, being in a high public trust." And "in the true spirit of the age . . . the disposition in the Judiciary should be strong to uphold them."

As applied after 1837, this rule changed constitutional federalism. The balance between state and national power, however, was not achieved by repudiating the nationalist doctrines of the Marshall Court but by applying them with qualifications and refusing to expand them. Thus, in the area of contract, the Court refused to extend the *Dartmouth College* ruling by implication, while Marshall, Story asserted, would have done so. Nor would the Court make the corporation into a full-fledged constitutional citizen as the corporate interests desired. The Court dropped from its legal arsenal the doctrine of implied limitations on state legislatures which had been taking shape gradually and tentatively under Marshall. Finally, in its interpretation of the commerce clause, the Court positively repudiated the idea of exclusive congressional power over commerce that Marshall had offered in the *Gibbons* opinion and tentatively employed in *Brown* v. *Maryland*. In contrast, the *Cooley* rule (*Cooley* v. *Board of Wardens,* 1852) was a practical compromise which preserved an area for state action without jeopardizing the power of Congress to act when circumstances demanded it. As a result of these changes, the federal system under Taney was pragmatic and untidy in comparison with that of Marshall's era—but it had history on its side. The absence of doctrine was as timely in law as in politics.

These modifications of constitutional nationalism neither destroyed the principles established by the Marshall Court nor disrupted the course of legal development or the stability of the Court itself. It continued to rely on the common law for substance and methodological guidance. Unworkable precedents like Marshall's *Deveaux* ruling and the tidewater limitation on admiralty jurisdiction were abruptly abandoned, but the existing law was modified only when required in a particular case and then without vindictiveness, speculation, or doctrinal exegesis.

Dependence on the work of former Courts was openly acknowledged. (As Story noted about Marshall's enduring influence, "Hardly a day now passes in the court he so dignified and adorned, without reference to some decision of his time as establishing a principle which, from that day to this, has been accepted as undoubted law. . . .") Instead of knocking down the Marshall Court, the new Court stood on its shoulders.

Nor did the Taney Court lay aside doctrinaire nationalism in order to pick up doctrinaire states' rights—though the pressure to do so was great both on and off the bench. No less than its predecessor, the Taney Court wanted to preserve national union. The difference was that the Taney Court understood that nationalist pronouncements from the bench could not by themselves cement the Union. For, in the last analysis, the union of the states rested on feelings of self-interest. By conceding the states enough power to satisfy self-interest within an increasingly diversified republic, the Court attempted to strengthen these essential bonds of nationalism. Such concessions to state-based self-interest were as necessary in the period after 1830 as they had been in 1787 or would be in 1877. Yet the Taney Court was also aware that the contact and mutual dependence which comes with national commerce had created the self-interest on which genuine union rested, and so it worked in behalf of national commerce too. But the Court was careful that its pronouncements of legal nationalism did not outrun nationalistic sentiment.

Division on the Taney Court pointed up the modification of the nationalism of Marshall's Court and the more balanced nature of the new federalism. John P. Frank's biography of Justice Daniel (*Justice Daniel Dissenting,* 1964) makes this point very effectively. On one end of the spectrum were Justices Story and McLean, who spoke for the constitutional nationalism of 1819. On the other were the Southern agrarians—Daniel of Virginia, Catron of Tennessee, and Campbell of Alabama—whose consistent dissents showed their disagreement with the policy of moderation. What they wanted—though they differed among themselves as to degree—were fewer concessions to corporate capitalism and more to states' rights. In a formal sense this group left hardly a ripple on the main stream of American jurisprudence. But through the prism of Southern agrarianism, they saw things their more moderate colleagues frequently missed. They perceived (what history was later to verify) that the business corporation was a revolutionary development in political and economic power which might hurt as well as help the public interest. In disagreeing with the Court's policy, they openly acknowledged that the Court was making policy, and, for this reason, they became vociferous spokesmen for judicial self-restraint. Unhappily for the Court and the nation, their insight could be dismissed as an apologia for slavery—for it was also that—and left outside the mainstream of judicial thought. Yet in the collective give and take on the Court, their persistent criticism affected the position of the moderate majority. For the historian, the agrarian states' rights philosophy behind these dissents provides a bench mark for measuring the distance between Jefferson's agrarian republic and the Taney Court, Jacksonian democracy, and the nineteenth century.

It was a tribute to Chief Justice Taney's leadership that these divisions, accompanied by conflicts of personality and the passions of conviction, did not immobilize the Court. When Webster bemoaned the absence of a great "leading mind" on the bench, he was overlooking the genius of Taney's leadership. There is abundant testimony (and Taney's biographers Carl Swisher and Walter Lewis [*Without Fear or Favor*, 1965] agree) that Taney in fact possessed that "intrinsic authority" which Frankfurter called the "test of leadership." But he did not use that authority to consolidate the Court or impose his own ideas upon it. Instead he recognized the inevitability of division and made a democratic virtue of necessity. By tact, innate gentleness, and infinite patience, he succeeded in moderating the personal conflict that accompanied disagreement— with one serious exception. In the resulting atmosphere of tolerance, he was able to bring together a majority that translated difference of opinion into constitutional moderation. Considering the obstacles, it was as impressive a feat of leadership as anything Marshall had done.

In the process of adjusting federalism to fit the new age, the Court itself assumed a new and historically appropriate posture. Not that the Court conceded its power of decision. New interpretations of the commerce clause and contracts left the Court's power of judicial review intact in those areas. Indeed in some fields—corporation, admiralty, maritime, and commercial law—the Court greatly expanded its jurisdiction. But its approach to power, its internal procedures, its methods, and its style differed from the Marshall Court's. Separate opinions, division, and dissent became regular occurrences. And, though not necessarily virtues in themselves, they reflected a new internal democracy which was congenial to a democratic age. Taney made it clear in the *Passenger Cases* that the Court might err but was free to change its mind when it found it had. And, appropriately, as it relaxed its imperial posture, the Court softened its magisterial rhetoric. Notions of natural law and constitutional finality gave way to a more realistic view of law as a process and the Court as an instrument of adjustment rather than an oracle of certitude.

To the great surprise of its detractors, the Court went up in popular reputation as it came down from the Olympian heights. Because it dealt moderately and respectfully with the work of the Marshall Court, it inherited the earlier Court's high reputation. By undertaking less and heeding Jacksonian priorities, the Court brought itself into harmony with the President and Congress (who in any case were not, as Richard Longaker reminds us in "Andrew Jackson and the Judiciary" [September, 1956], raging anti-Court demons). Consequently, by 1850, the national prestige of the Court was as great as in the golden days of Marshall.

But if the Supreme Court is ever composed of imprudent or bad men, the Union may be plunged into anarchy or civil war.

ALEXIS DE TOCQUEVILLE (1835)

FIVE

The Court's Time of Troubles: Slavery, Sectionalism, and War

Had the Taney Court retired on its laurels in 1856, it would surely have gone down as one of the most popular and effective Courts in our history. Taney's tactful leadership, his simple eloquence, and the clarity of his legal mind would have assured his reputation as a worthy successor to the great Marshall. But a Negro slave called Dred caused the Court and its Chief

Justice to lose this commendation. In a single decision, the Court abandoned its moderation, threw away its popularity, and jeopardized its very institutional existence. Instead of a great judicial statesman, Roger Taney became a "mere man," as one Northern paper called him, or, in a less generous appraisal, a minion of Southern slavocracy and denigrator of the Marshall tradition.

It is a paradox that slavery should have become so important a factor in appraising the Court's statesmanship—as well as the main focus of historiographical concern—for, by ordinary standards, that issue was peripheral to the Court's work. Of all the cases decided by the Marshall and Taney Courts, hardly more than a hundred dealt with slavery, and most of those did so indirectly. Only a handful of these cases are remembered; not one, including *Dred Scott* v. *Sanford* (unless one counts the unintended lesson on judicial humility), contributed any lasting principle to American law. However, more than any other issue, slavery raised crucial constitutional and strategic questions which put judicial statesmanship to the supreme test: the Court had to deal with the demarcation of state and national power and also face the limits of its own lawmaking role.

Slavery was bound to come before the Court. It was basic to the political and economic life of half the states of the Union, and the Court was obliged to recognize the laws of these states. Slavery was part (the *major* part, argues Staughton Lynd in *Class Conflict, Slavery, and the United States Constitution*, 1968) of the constitutional compromise which made the Union possible; as such it was part of the supreme law of the land. The bargain between "the great northern and southern interests," to use Madison's words, included guarantees that Congress would not tax slaves directly or interfere with the slave trade for twenty years. Three-fifths of the slaves were to be counted for purposes of taxation and apportionment of representatives. Escaped slaves, it was promised, would be returned. On the subject of slavery in the new territories and states, the Constitution was conveniently obscure. All that was said was that Congress might "make all needful rules and regulations" respecting territories, and each section assumed that a continued "spirit of accommodation" would resolve constitutional ambiguity in its favor.

Unhappily for the Court, developments in the antebellum period were all working against the slavery compromise of 1787. Not only did that arrangement become progressively less satisfactory, but slavery came to subsume and to symbolize the whole range of political, economic, and moral differences between the sections. The process began as the exploitative spirit in both the North and the South fulfilled the economic logic of climatic and geographic differences. Encouraged by the cotton gin, new types of cotton seed, and rising prices, the South made cotton and slavery the economic basis of its society. And soil exhaustion, augmented by the expansionist impulse, carried cotton culture into the deep South. In the North, industrial capitalism replaced agriculture and commercial capitalism as the dynamic economic force. On these contrary economic foundations, each section erected a distinctive culture—one tending to corporateness and conservatism, the other to individualism and liberalism. The Panic of 1819 and the Missouri Debates helped turn sectional differences into sectional self-consciousness, and the militant abolitionism of the 1830's changed this into a sectional narcissism which defined the Union and the good life in strictly sectional terms. And at precisely the time that the North and South were growing economically and psychologically apart, they were thrown into unavoidable contact by the transportation and communications revolution of the 1840's and competition for control of the West.

Since it was loaded with the political and economic and also the moral burden of sectional antagonism, the constitutional issue of slavery was fatefully contrived to test the Court. Impelled by its declining national power, the South turned to states' rights to defend slavery, and once again the Court was faced with the task of adjusting the division of power between state and nation. This time judicial error would certainly not be tolerated. The new and crucial factor here was that the adjustment had to be one which satisfied the political and economic imperatives of the sections but at the same time did not

offend the morality of the majority of the American people—
for the authority of the law and of the Court depended finally
on the good will of this majority. By the 1850's, moral indifference to slavery, which had permitted the constitutional settlement of 1787, had turned into zealous abolitionism in the
North. The fact that Northern morality was partly hypocritical
and a luxury of economic self-interest did not concern judicial
strategy; it was sufficient that it represented the morality of the
majority. In retrospect, it seems clear that the Court could not
have gotten away with using an extrapolation of the slavery
compromise of 1787 for its constitutional solution.

THE COURT AND SLAVERY

Most slavery cases before the Court afforded little opportunity
for either policy-making or judicial miscalculation. Most of
them came from the states and turned on questions of state
law—which is to say that the Court was obliged to treat the
slave as property. Reduced to a chattel, the Negro was disposed
of in wills, deeds, mortgages, bills, and notes in the dry language and the strict formal rules of the common law. Cases
arising under the several congressional statutes regulating, and,
in 1819, prohibiting, the foreign slave trade permitted only a
little more creative leeway. Judicial interpretation of those laws
was essential to their enforcement, however, and cases involving them cast the Court in a more favorable moral light than
the cases arising under state law. Occasionally the gross evils of
the slave trade would tempt a judge to abandon legal techni-
cality for the morality of natural justice. Judge Story's circuit
opinion in *United States* v. *Le Jeune Eugenie* (1822), for
example, won the praise of rising anti-slave forces because of
its condemnation of the slave trade and, by implication, slavery
itself as "repugnant to the great principles of Christian duty,
the dictates of natural religion, the obligations of good faith
and morality, and the eternal maxims of social justice." The
majority of the Supreme Court resisted Story's moral solution,
and, in *The Antelope* (1825), Marshall reminded his colleague
that his noble sentiments had nothing to do with international

law. Despite congressional prohibition and judicial enforcement, the slave trade continued until the Civil War—with a large share of the profits going North.

It was questions of commerce rather than the slave trade which gave the Court the chance to deal with slavery. If the definition of the national commerce power included slave and free Negroes within the meaning of commerce, then state control over slavery would be weakened at several vital points. One such point was Southern state police laws prohibiting the entrance of free Negroes into the state in the interest of social order. Some justices insisted on grappling with the issue. On circuit in 1823, Justice Johnson "hung himself on a democratic snag," as Marshall put it, by striking down one such South Carolina law as an encroachment on the power of Congress to regulate commerce—a ruling which the state completely ignored. *Groves* v. *Slaughter* (1841) raised the question of whether the section of the Mississippi Constitution which prohibited the importation or sale of slaves unlawfully encroached on Congress' power to regulate commerce. Justices Taney, McLean, and Daniel were tempted to grapple directly with the explosive issue. A more cautious majority, however, skirted the whole problem by holding that the constitutional prohibition had not been implemented by necessary legislative action. In *New York* v. *Miln* and the *License* and *Passenger Cases,* the crucial question was whether and to what extent congressional power over commerce embraced persons (in this case slaves and free Negroes) and limited state control over their movement across state lines. The question permeated judicial reasoning and contributed to judicial indecision. On occasion, it was openly discussed, but both the confusion in the early commerce decisions and the calculated moderation of the later decisions worked to keep the issue submerged most of the time.

THE FUGITIVE SLAVE QUESTION

As long as the Court could deal with slavery and not the Negro slave, as long as it could talk of bills and notes, deeds and statutory interpretation, and not humanity, it could avoid arousing moral fervor and dividing the popular opinion on which its authority rested. All that came to an end in 1841 because the black man persisted in escaping the law that made him somebody's property.

The fugitives in *United States* v. *Schooner Amistad* (1841) were not American slaves but Africans on their way to enslavement. They had other ideas and, on June 30, 1839, en route to Puerto Principo, Cuba, they rose up, killed the ship's captain, and forced two Spanish slavers to steer the ship back to Africa. However, the Spaniards directed the *Amistad* to United States waters, where she was seized by the United States brig *Washington*. The officers and crew brought the Negroes into the federal district court in Connecticut and filed a libel claiming salvage. By the time the case reached the Supreme Court, it had gone far beyond the question of salvage and treaty rights under which the Spanish owners claimed the Africans. As counsel for the Negroes put it, the issue was that of "humble Africans" asserting their right to be free men against the machinations of two powerful governments. Former President John Quincy Adams returned to the bar of the Court and was, as Justice Baldwin put it, "charged to the muzzle" with moral indignation. Forgetting his seventy-four years (and often the legal issues before the Court) he spent three days in powerful and bitterly sarcastic argument in an effort to get the moral issue across to the Court and the nation. Justice Story's deliberately restrained opinion, which used principles of municipal and international law for freeing the Africans, did not avert a sectional response. Northerners, who were not put off by the Court's moderation, rallied to its defense of freedom; the South looked on and drew dark conclusions from the North's enthusiastic reaction.

One year later, before the passions of the *Amistad* case had subsided, the Court faced the domestic fugitive slave problem in *Prigg* v. *Pennsylvania* (1842). This time the spirit of comity that sustained the slavery compromise was severely strained. Professional slave-catcher Edward Prigg had been sent to Pennsylvania by a Maryland owner to recover an alleged slave, Margaret Morgan. Prigg caught the woman and returned her to Maryland with her newborn baby. He was thereupon indicted in the Pennsylvania courts for violation of that state's personal liberty law, which established procedural safeguards in rendition cases. The question which put the Court in such a difficult position was whether Pennsylvania's law violated the constitutional guarantee of fugitive slave return and the 1793 Act of Congress passed to implement it. Maryland and the South viewed the Pennsylvania law as a palpable deprivation of their constitutionally guaranteed property rights. Pennsylvania and the North, relying on the ambiguity about a state's obligations to return fugitives, demanded the right to pass laws protecting free Negroes from the incursions of slave-catchers.

Justice Story improvised brilliantly in order to please both sections. He said the Pennsylvania law was a violation of the clear, constitutional, statutory obligation to return fugitives; the majority of the Court concurred and the South cheered. But the cheering stopped—and Taney, Daniel, and Thompson dissented—when Story declared that power over fugitives belonged exclusively to the national government. There is real doubt whether Story carried a majority on his exclusivist argument, and when he went on to say that the Northern states were not obliged to, indeed could not constitutionally, assist in the return of slaves, he lost the support of the majority. Extremists in both sections abused the Court: Southern firebrands for not going the whole distance with slavery; their Northern counterparts for going too far. (William Lloyd Garrison proposed immediate Northern withdrawal from the Union, and the Massachusetts Anti-Slavery Society reckoned that an "overthrow of the Constitution and the government" might be necessary.) Moderate Southerners settled for the immediate victory and the judicial assurance of their constitutional rights. Most Northern criticism subsided in the belief that the burden of state compliance with the 1793 statute had been lifted, and six Northern states passed laws prohibiting such compliance.

In avoiding one crisis the Court prepared the way for a greater one. By discouraging state cooperation in returning fugitives, the *Prigg* decision undercut the Fugitive Slave Act of

1793 and made necessary the more brutal one of 1850. The South had been forced to look to the federal government for a national solution, and the Court pledged itself in advance to support such a solution, despite the fact that the North would certainly be mobilized against it. And people began to think of the Court as uniquely constituted to quell the agitation over slavery. Willy-nilly the Court had left its sanctuary of non-involvement, entered the political thicket of slavery, and unwittingly taken the first step toward the disaster of *Dred Scott*.

Reaction to the *Amistad* and *Prigg* decisions reminded the Court—if indeed it needed reminding—that involvement on either side of the fugitive slave issue would take a heavy toll of its popularity. Accordingly, when there was a way out, as in *Strader* v. *Graham* (1851), the Court took it. That case dealt with the touchy problem of whether slaves who had visited Ohio and returned to Kentucky became free men by virtue of the laws of Ohio and the Ordinance of 1787. In a unanimous opinion, the Court refused jurisdiction on the ground that the Kentucky law was controlling and no federal question was involved. Had the Court followed this tactic six years later in the *Dred Scott* case, some have insisted, the history of the republic might have been different.

There were many cases prosecuted under the Fugitive Slave Acts of 1793 and 1850, however, in which the Court and the justices on circuit could not escape their responsibilities. And the Court, Northern and anti-slave justices included, did its onerous duty for the slaveholders in these cases. Northern Justice Levi Woodbury explained the Court's premise in *Jones* v. *Van Zandt* (1849), when he reminded the nation that the Constitution had struck a bargain with slavery, and the Court had no recourse but to "go where that constitution and the laws lead, and not to break both, by travelling without or beyond them." Even when the Northern states resorted to the states' rights doctrines of Calhoun and the anti-Court prejudices of Jefferson, the Court persisted. Indeed, in *Ableman* v. *Booth* (1859), it put down state resistance to enforcement of the fugitive slave law with an assertion of judicial nationalism that surpassed pronouncements by Marshall and Story forty years earlier.

THAT "BLACK QUESTION": SLAVERY IN THE TERRITORIES

The fugitive slave problem aroused bitter sectional feeling, but it was the question of slavery in the territories that fully—and fatally as it turned out—joined the issue between the North and the South. The South considered the right to extend slavery basic to its future existence. The constant acquisition of new land was an economic imperative for the slave economy, the *sine qua non* of Southern agrarian capitalism. The admission of new slave states would also bolster the declining political strength of the South, especially in the Senate. And Southern honor demanded the right as a reward for its services to the Union and as an indication of the good intentions of the North. But the North was not in an obliging mood. Convinced that slavery and free labor were incompatible and that it had a moral duty to make the nation over in its own image, the North insisted the new territories should be free. And, since the North also possessed a numerical, political, and economic preponderance, it was not inclined to temper its demand. Here, then, was the explosive political issue which the Supreme Court boldly undertook to solve in 1857. To understand why the Court took up the *Dred Scott* case and to appreciate fully the disastrous impact of the decision, a quick review of the political history of the territorial problem is in order.

Despite their importance, the territories occupied an anomalous position in American government, lying in a sort of constitutional no man's land between the states and the federal government. (This is shown by Arthur Bestor in his superb analysis of the problem, "State Sovereignty and Slavery: A Reinterpretation of Proslavery Constitutional Doctrine, 1846–1860," Summer, 1961.) The ambiguous locus of power was not important in most territorial matters, but it did have an effect on the slavery question. For, as the South and North well knew, any decision about slavery during the territorial phase of a state would mark the new state as slave or free and would shape the balance of sectional power in the Union as well. And because it was so crucial to sectional harmony, the status of slavery in the territories was treated with more than the usual vagueness in the Constitution. Neither the debates nor the ratifying conventions specified whether Article IV, Section 3, the grant of power authorizing Congress to make all needful rules and regulations for the territories, included the power to control and possibly prohibit slavery there. But political logic strongly suggested that Congress, which possessed the machinery of compromise for patching together a legislative solution to territorial problems as they arose, should have the power to act. In fact, Congress immediately assumed the power and used it to keep sectional peace. Justice B. R. Curtis counted fourteen instances of congressional legislation on the question between 1789 and 1848: six of these acts—all before 1822—had recognized and continued slavery; eight had followed the precedent of the Northwest Ordinance and prohibited it. (The most important of these, of course, was the Compromise of 1820 which excluded slavery from the entire Louisiana Purchase territory north of 36° 30′, excepting Missouri.) Even if Curtis' tally was a bit imprecise, it demonstrated beyond doubt that Congress had power over slavery in the territories and that it had, as a matter of course, used that power to strike a North-South balance. So far as the Court said anything on the subject, mainly in *American Insurance Co.* v. *Canter* (1828), it supported congressional power. Presidents from Washington through John Quincy Adams did the same.

After the Missouri Compromise, however, circumstances undercut both the spirit of congressional compromise and the theory of congressional power on which it rested. In the 1830's, debate over the admission of Texas, coming on top of abolitionism and arguments over the right of petition, burdened the territorial question with the full weight of sectional antagonism. The Mexican War, fought to validate the annexation of Texas and to lay claim to more Mexican territory, seemed to the North the final culmination of a "planter conspiracy" to control the West. The South, on the other hand, viewed David Wilmot's 1846 resolution banning slavery permanently from any territory acquired from Mexico as evidence of the North's intentions to use its preponderance in Congress to deny Southern rights in the new lands. The South was disturbed because the resolution broke with the custom of equitable distribution, not because it called on congressional power.

With extremism rampant in the North and the South, Congress was hard put to satisfy sectional demands regarding the Mexican cession—and was increasingly less interested in having the power to do so. While Congress held back, extremists from both sections expounded constitutional theory to support their own interests (as De Tocqueville had said they would). Reminded of its declining congressional power by the passage of the Wilmot Proviso in the House, the South began to question how much control Congress should have over the territories and became more insistent on guarantees of its constitutional right to extend slavery. As this demand was refined into a states' rights doctrine, it laid a constitutional burden on Congress, the agent of the states, to protect slavery during the territorial stage. Anti-slavery Northerners were willing to accept congressional power as long as it worked for them. When it did not, they turned to their own view of the Constitution and, failing that, to a still "higher law." With the decline in congressional effectiveness, and with both the North and South demanding a definitive solution—within the Constitution if possible, outside it if necessary—the stage was set for the Court's entrance.

Yet there was a way out which might satisfy Northern and Southern moderates, take Congress off the hook, and save the Court from getting involved. It lay in the ambiguous idea of popular sovereignty, somewhere between the absolute theories of the extremists. Founded on the "great fundamental principle of self-government," as Senator Stephen Douglas noted whenever he got the chance, popular sovereignty left the people of the territories "free to form and regulate their domestic institutions in their own way, subject only to the Constitution of the United States." What did the Constitution require? When would the settlers act? By what political mechanism? With what finality? The beauty of popular sovereignty was that no one really knew, and everyone could read his own self-serving interpretation into the confusion. The one sure thing was that Congress—and, of course, the national political parties—would be relieved of the obligation to act without having surrendered the theoretical power to do so.

By applying the pragmatic formula of popular sovereignty —the decision not to decide—Congress attempted to dispose of the territorial questions of the 1850's. In 1850, in accord with Clay's compromise resolution of that year, the territories of New Mexico and Utah were organized without congressional restrictions on slavery and with the settlers having the right to decide the slavery issues themselves. Four years later, popular sovereignty was applied to the territories of Kansas and Nebraska, and it was here that it was put to the crucial test. Both territories lay within the upper reaches of the Louisiana Purchase and, by the terms of the Missouri Compromise, would have been organized as free territories. Would have, that is, except for the influence of sectional, railroad, and presidential politics. Senator Stephen Douglas of Illinois wanted the transcontinental railroad to go through Chicago, and if Kansas and Nebraska became territories, the Chicago route had a better chance. Also, as an aspirant for the Democratic nomination for the Presidency, Douglas favored a compromise solution to the territorial problem which would hold the Northern and Southern wings of his party together. Popular sovereignty served both ends. By applying the principle of self-determination to Kansas and Nebraska rather than the Compromise of 1820, Douglas could win over the Southern opposition in the Senate. Popular sovereignty could also provide a rallying ground for the disintegrating Democratic party. Accordingly, the Kansas-Nebraska Act of May, 1854, declared "inoperative and void" the 36°30′ provision of the Missouri Compromise and introduced in its place the "principle of non-intervention by Congress with slavery in the States and Territories." Instead of having Congress guarantee free territories, the people of the territories were now given the dubious privilege of choosing for themselves.

Pro- and anti-slave settlers in Kansas implemented the vague formula by killing one another and dividing the territory into two armed camps, one slave and one free. The turmoil in Kansas split the Democrats in Congress along sectional lines, with Senator Douglas and the moderates desperately laboring to make enough sense out of popular sovereignty to reunite the party. At the same time, a new sectional party called the Republicans, which opposed slavery in the territories, forged unity from the flames of Kansas and waited to pick up the reins of power which the divided Democrats would drop.

ENTER DRED SCOTT

At the height of the Kansas crisis, with extremism rampant and the national party structure tottering, President Buchanan casually dropped a bombshell in his inaugural address, March 4, 1857. Admitting, in what was surely the understatement of the decade, that the "happy conception" of popular sovereignty had raised some questions, he went on confidently to promise that they were of "little practical importance." In any event, the whole thing was "a judicial question" which was about to be "speedily and finally settled." The President knew whereof he spoke. The case of *Dred Scott* v. *Sanford,* which had been on the Court's docket since 1854, was decided two days after the inaugural promise.

To understand the Court's daring entrance into the high politics of the republic, it is necessary to recount the journeys of a Negro slave called Dred Scott, as well as his aspirations for freedom. Scott was the property of Dr. John Emerson, a surgeon in the United States Army and a resident of Missouri. Emerson took his slave with him on a tour of duty in the Northwest—to Fort Armstrong in the free state of Illinois in 1834 and in 1836 to Fort Snelling in the upper Louisiana Purchase territory, which had become free under the Missouri Compromise. In 1838 Emerson removed Scott, who now had a wife and baby daughter, to Missouri. Emerson died in 1843, willing the Scott family to his widow. After an unsuccessful effort to purchase freedom for himself and his family, Dred Scott sued in the low state court of Missouri, arguing that residence in a free state and territory had made him free. The Scotts (his wife's case was a companion suit) won their freedom in the lower court only to lose it before the Missouri Supreme Court. Caught up in the state's bitter slavery politics, that court went against the strong current of previous Missouri decisions by ruling that the slavery prohibition in the Missouri Compromise and the laws of Illinois had no extraterritorial effect in Missouri. When Scott returned to Missouri, the slave law of that state determined his status.

Had Scott's lawyer Roswell Field followed the customary procedure at this point—taken the case on a writ of error from the state court to the Supreme Court—he might have changed the course of history. If this legal maneuver had been used, the Supreme Court would have been bound (according to *Strader* v. *Graham,* 1851, and other cases) by the decision of the Missouri Supreme Court, and would have had to deny jurisdiction. To avoid just this result, Field brought the case into the federal circuit court for the district of Missouri in November, 1853—while the first litigation was still pending in the lower Missouri Court where it had been remanded—on diversity of citizenship jurisdiction. As a citizen of Missouri, Scott, the argument went, was suing Sanford * (as executor of Mr. Emerson's will), a citizen of New York, for assault. Otherwise, the evidence and arguments in support of Scott's freedom were identical to those used in the state courts.

Sanford pleaded to the jurisdiction of the court, contending that since Dred Scott was a "negro of African descent," he was not a citizen of the United States capable of suing in the federal courts. Scott demurred to this plea, i.e., admitted that he was an African Negro but argued that this did not bar him from citizenship and the right to sue. Sanford pleaded over or accepted the issue as joined and the circuit court ruled, on the

---

* "Sanford" is the correct spelling, but the name was spelled "Sandford" in the Reports.

basis of his residence and ownership of property, that Scott was a citizen capable of suing in the federal courts. On the merits, however, the court agreed with the state supreme court that the Missouri Compromise and the laws of Illinois were not controlling and so instructed the jury, which brought in the verdict that Dred Scott was a slave by state law. The case then went to the Supreme Court on a writ of error; it was docketed in December, 1854, argued first in February, 1856, reargued after conference in December, 1856, and finally decided on March 6, 1857. Since the case came from the lower federal court rather than the state court, the whole range of questions concerning slavery in the territories was technically before the Court—if it were bold enough to review them.

It was. In nine separate opinions (two in dissent) covering 234 pages, the justices set out to rescue the republic. The Chief Justice's opinion was referred to, somewhat generously, by the Court reporter as "the opinion of the Court." After establishing the Court's technical right, indeed duty, to consider all aspects of the case, Taney turned to the question of citizenship for the first time in the Court's history.

The initial and controlling question was whether Dred Scott was a citizen with the constitutional right to sue in the federal courts. The Circuit Court for the District of Missouri had ruled in favor of Scott's right to sue, but it did not elaborate on the meaning of citizenship. In view of the Supreme Court's willingness to concede citizenship to corporations for the purpose of suing, one might have anticipated a rule in agreement with the lower court. But the Chief Justice emphatically said no. And he gave a definition of citizenship to support his negative decision. There were, he said, two separate categories of citizenship, one state and the other national. State citizenship was municipal and conferred no rights beyond the state in which it was granted; specifically, it could not confer the right to sue in federal courts. National citizenship was controlled by the Constitution itself. The document of 1787, asserted Taney, introducing the racist argument linked with his name for years to come, bluntly recognized a "perpetual and impassible barrier" between whites and blacks and considered the latter "subjugated by the former," a "subordinate and inferior class of being" with no rights except ones which "those who held the power and the government might choose to give them." Though the Negro might be free, or even a state citizen, he and his descendants could not be citizens of the United States within the meaning of the Constitution. As for a Negro who was also a slave, he could not by definition be a citizen and had no access to federal courts. Dred Scott was a Negro and possibly still a slave; he could not, therefore, sue in the courts of the nation.

So far as Dred Scott was concerned the case was over. Neither the circuit court nor the Supreme Court could rule on his argument for freedom; the Supreme Court of Missouri's decision against him stood as law. Presumably, then, the Chief Justice might have stopped with his ruling on jurisdiction. Instead, he intrepidly went on to consider the substance of Scott's argument and the explosive issue of slavery in the territories that it raised. Dred Scott contended he was free by virtue of his residence in the upper Louisiana Territory (later to be Minnesota) made free by the Missouri Compromise. The fundamental question was whether Congress had had authority to prohibit slavery in that territory in the first place—and Taney took this question up. The Constitution, he observed, did not give Congress plenary power over the territories. The "needful rules and regulations" clause of Article IV, Section 3, and Marshall's opinion in the *American Insurance Company* case (1828), usually cited in support of such congressional power, were inadequate authorities. The former applied only to territories already possessed by the government in 1787; the latter applied only to the Florida territory. Indeed, far from granting plenary power, the Constitution imposed severe limitations on congressional authority over the territories. And here the Chief Justice introduced the Southern states' rights theory which had taken shape in response to the Wilmot Proviso. The federal government might acquire territory and govern it, he conceded. But when it did, it acted as the trustee of the people of the several states and for their common benefit. And, whatever Congress did in the territories, it must respect the rights of persons and property of the citizens of the states, not excluding those Southern states which recognized slaves as property. This obligation, continued Taney, was not left to inference. He was referring to the clause of the Fifth Amendment which prohibited the government from depriving persons of life, liberty, and property without due process of law. As it had been understood, this clause did not confer the absolute rights of life, liberty, or property; it held only that those rights could not be abridged except according to established processes of law. Taney shifted the meaning from procedure to substance. Congress, he declared categorically, could not deprive persons of property; since slaves were property, it could not prohibit slavery in the territories. The 36° 30′ provision of the Missouri Compromise, therefore, had been unconstitutional and Scott's argument concerning his residence in free territory had no validity. His further claim that he was free by virtue of residence in the free state of Illinois, Taney added, was answered by *Strader* v. *Graham*. The Court ruled in that case that the status of slaves who had resided in a free state and returned to a slave state was determined exclusively by the laws of the latter. Whatever Dred Scott's status had been in Illinois, he became a slave on his return to Missouri.

The Chief Justice had spoken. But how much of his opinion was law was obscured by the Court's uncertainty as to what questions were legitimately before it and by the chaos of the separate opinions. The initial legal question was whether the Court, after having concluded that it had no jurisdiction because Dred Scott was not a national citizen, could still rule on the merits of the question—i.e., did Congress have the power to prohibit slavery in the territories. Contemporary critics and many historians since have declared that Taney's opinion beyond the ruling on jurisdiction was obiter dictum. However, Corwin ("The Dred Scott Decision in the Light of Contemporary Legal Doctrine," October, 1911) and Hagan ("The Dred Scott Decision," January, 1926) have shown that the Court was technically entitled to consider all the questions, since, as Taney himself explained, the writ of error issued to the lower federal and not the state court. It was, in fact, logically im-

pelled to broaden the scope of its inquiry, because the jurisdictional issue was inextricably bound up with a consideration
of Scott's arguments for his freedom. For unless he were free
he could not presume to be a citizen of Missouri capable of
suing in the federal courts. In pursuing the jurisdictional question, then, Taney was carried on to a consideration of the
substance of the case. Once there, he could not, as some
critics suggest, have settled the questions by reliance on *Strader
v. Graham,* since it applied only to that part of the argument
dealing with residence in a free state. The effect of residence
in a free territory on Scott's status was a separate question
requiring a separate answer.

Conceding that Taney's approach was justified by law and
logic, however, still leaves the position of the Court unclear.
Six judges denied Congress had the power to prohibit slavery
in the territories. But, as only three of those thought the
question fairly before the Court, it is doubtful that the Court
decided any law on that crucial point. The problem was reversed on the question of Negro citizenship. Here Taney's
opinion had the support of only three justices, a point which
is obscured by the fact that, in the opinions of five justices,
the question was referred to as "decided" by the Court. Piecing
the opinions together, one careful scholar concludes that
nothing was clear except that Dred Scott remained a slave and
therefore was not a citizen and that the Court had no jurisdiction (see Frederick S. Allis, Jr., "The Dred Scott Labyrinth," in
H. Stuart Hughes, ed., *Teachers of History: Essays in Honor of
Laurence Bradford Packard,* 1954).

Justice McLean and Justice Curtis both dissented in separate opinions. Curtis' opinion was taken as the conclusive
statement of the minority position because of its scholarship
and clarity of argument. After admonishing the Court for its
lack of restraint, Curtis refuted Taney's opinion point by point.
First, national citizenship followed state citizenship and, he
noted, as early as 1787 five states had conferred citizenship
on Negroes. Second, Congress had consistently exercised authority over slavery in the territories with the Court's support,
and prescription was recognized by the Court as evidence of

constitutionality. Finally, a correct appreciation of the rules governing conflict of law between states, as well as a correct understanding of Missouri law, would show that Scott retained his freedom on his return to Missouri. The anti-slave forces forgot their earlier deprecation of Curtis for upholding the fugitive slave law. Even before the delivery of the Court's opinion, they printed and circulated his opinion as the true law of the Constitution.

Rarely has the Court undertaken so much—but settled so little. Taney's doctrine of dual citizenship was ignored in the Northern lower federal courts as soon as it was expounded; in 1868, the Fourteenth Amendment laid it to rest for good. The Court's settlement of the territorial question was neither final nor controlling: Section 8 of the Missouri Compromise, which the Court voided, had already been repealed by Congress. Free Soilers in Kansas settled their problem without reference to *Dred Scott* by voting down the pro-slave constitution of 1858 and entering the Union as a free state in 1861. The Republican Party platform of 1860, based on the prohibition of slavery in the territories, casually overlooked the decision. So did Congress in June, 1862, when it outlawed slavery in all existing territories without compensation. Even the Court's determination of Scott's fate was reversed three months later when Calvin Chaffee, the abolitionist husband of Widow Emerson, manumitted the Scott family. To be sure, the post-Civil War Court cited Taney's opinion in support of the emerging substantive interpretation of the Fifth and Fourteenth Amendments. But that interpretation, given the Court's congeniality to the imperative of the new age, did not depend on precedent. It is even doubtful that the *Dred Scott* decision advanced the doctrine of judicial review of congressional acts. To be sure, it was the second time the Court had nullified an act of Congress and the first time an act not dealing with the judicial branch was involved. But the decision did more to jeopardize judicial power than any decision the Court has ever made.

The results of the decision were far reaching and deleterious. The Court's hard-won prestige dissolved immediately. Personal division among the judges—so bitter that Justice

Curtis resigned—became a matter of public gossip. The opinions were so numerous and diffuse that not even the profession was certain what law had been decided. (It was even rumored, and was probably true, that Taney had added several pages of argument to his opinion after it had been read in Court and before it was printed.) The nation was in no mind to pick legal bones, however, and it accepted Taney's pro-slave opinion as the law. A few who supported the administration and some Southerners came to the defense of the Court. But Northern newspapers, congressmen, and state legislators endorsed popular opinion by heaping abuse on the decision and the Court that had made it.

In the eyes of the North, the justices had become "mere men," and the Court's majority—"five slaveholders and two doughfaces," Greeley's *Tribune* called them—were agents in a plot to aggrandize the South. On the Senate floor, William Seward charged conspiracy between Buchanan and the pro-slave justices, and Lincoln expanded the cabal to include "Stephen [Douglas], Franklin [Pierce], Roger [Taney], and James [Buchanan]." An opinion so contrived, asserted the *Tribune,* was entitled to "just so much moral weight as would be the judgment of those congregated in any Washington barroom." With its reputation at this new low, with cries for basic reform coming from all directions, the Court confronted the constitutional crisis of the Civil War.

Dred Scott damaged, for better or for worse, the machinery of political compromise even more than it did the Court. The decision made the position of the Republican party (whose *raison d'être* was opposition to slavery in the territories) constitutionally impossible; it was forced to denounce the Court, strengthening abolitionist sentiment within party ranks. As for the Democratic party—the only national party and the sole institution for compromise—its fate depended on its Northern and Southern factions accepting popular sovereignty. But, as Lincoln put it to Douglas at Freeport, Illinois, if the Constitution and the Supreme Court prohibited both Congress and the territorial legislatures from excluding slavery, by what authority could the settlers themselves do so? Perhaps they could, Senator Douglas responded, by refusing to pass the police legislation necessary to enforce slavery. This refined logic failed to allay Northern misgivings. And, even if the Northern Democrats had accepted popular sovereignty, how could the Southern Democrats be expected to forgo the certain advantage of *Dred Scott* for the contingency of a popular decision? When they refused at the national convention at Charlestown in 1860, the Democratic party split and hope for political compromise faded. By bolstering slavery with constitutional law, the Court forced the North to go beyond the Constitution and the South to reject it as a worthless promise. And without the Constitution, there was nothing left but the grim logic of marching men.

PITFALLS OF JUDICIAL DISCRETION

When the Court decided *Dred Scott,* it put itself on trial. And historians soon rushed in with a collection of opinions so various in scope, merit, and conclusion as to confound analysis. (Stanley Kutler's edition of primary and contemporary materials in *The Dred Scott Decision* [1967], with the interpretive guidance of F. S. Allis, Jr.'s "The Dred Scott Labyrinth," is an excellent starting point for understanding the welter of views.) Whether historians have referred to the decision tolerantly as an "error in judgment" or harshly as "judicial egoism" or a "monstrous piece of judicial effrontery," their general verdict is that the Court exceeded its bounds and undertook what was judicially impossible. Viewed as a case study of the nature and limitations of judicial power—which is the most profitable approach and the one most commonly found in recent scholarship—*Dred Scott* has much to offer. There are many puzzling points: Why, at the peak of its popularity, after skillfully navigating the troubled sea of federalism for twenty years, did the Court head into the treacherous political realm of slavery in the territories? Why, once it was there, did the justices decide as they did? Were they "mere men," "bad" men, or merely "imprudent" ones?

History's harsh verdict rests on the fact that the Court need not have become involved in the political crisis at all—though existing arguments in support of this point miss the mark. The contention that all the Court had to do was to behave legally (i.e., refuse to consider the case on its merits) is erroneous: as we have seen, the Court was justified and logically compelled to consider the whole question. But to conclude that it therefore had to do so is to choose the science over the art of judicial statesmanship. Since the days of Marshall anyhow, the Court has been able to employ calculated vagueness in times of crisis. That something less than a comprehensive and lucid treatment of the *Scott* case was possible is obvious from the Court's early conference decision to ignore both law and logic by affirming the circuit court decision below, thus escaping the question of slavery in the territories. Justice Nelson was appointed to write such an opinion for the majority and did in fact do so, relying heavily on *Strader* v. *Graham*. He delivered it finally as his own opinion but with the majority "we" still intact. It could hardly have been more confusing if the resulting inexactitude had been intended. To put it another way, the real blunder was not that the "opinion of the Court" was hopelessly confused, but that it seemed clear.

What drew the Court from the path of expediency into the arena of politics? A pro-slave conspiracy composed of the President, Democratic congressmen, and the "black robes," said the North. And, with a selective use of evidence, a persuasive case can be made to support this: The opinions followed sectional lines. The five Southern justices, joined by those "two doughfaces" from New York and Pennsylvania, where pro-Southern sentiments were strong, were ranged against those from Ohio and Massachusetts, centers of abolitionism. The argument against Dred Scott had been conducted by Reverdy Johnson, a close friend of the Chief Justice, who, it was said, pressured Taney to decide as he did. (Northern advocates of conspiracy conveniently ignored the fact that Justice Curtis' brother was counsel for Scott.) President Buchanan, whose pro-slavery sympathies were evident in his Kansas policy, wrote letters to Justices Catron and Grier urging a judicial solution. Assurance came in Catron's return letter. The hundreds who saw the President and the Chief Justice chatting confidentially before the inaugural announcement drew the easy conclusion that Buchanan's subsequent promise of a judicial solution meant that it was rigged. The Court's enforcement of the fugitive slave law, the repeal of the Missouri Compromise in 1854, and the Court's pronouncement of it as void in 1857 prepared the North to believe the worst—which it did.

The worst, however, was wrong. The Court was imprudent perhaps but not conspiratorial. An intricate combination of general and specific factors accounts for its imprudence. High on the list was the determination of Justices McLean and Curtis to explore the whole question despite the early majority decision in conference to escape the problem via the *Strader* precedent. Both were moved by conviction, but McLean had a personal motive as well. To get the Republican presidential nomination in 1856—which he desperately wanted—McLean needed to publicize his anti-slavery views. It was in fact to prevent just this that the case was postponed for reargument until after the November elections, but McLean broadcast his views on the territorial question through the newspapers anyhow.

Even the prospect of two dissents might not have moved the Court from its moderate course, however, had there not been among the justices a latent desire to stamp out, as fatal to the Union, the radical anti-Court, anti-Constitutional notions of the abolitionists. These now appeared to have invaded the temple in the persons of McLean and Curtis. All the Court needed was assurance that it could do the job of eradication successfully. Unfortunately, there was much to encourage this prideful conclusion. After all, the Court was at the apogee of its prestige among moderates in both sections. Statesmen— including at one time or another Lincoln, Clay, Douglas, Webster, and Presidents Pierce and Buchanan—and leaders of the bar were increasingly intrigued with a judicial cure for the nation's illness. This inclination was, in turn, fortified by a tendency of the age to fall back in emergencies on the Constitution, which, while it was being threatened, became even more venerable. Most important (and Wallace Mendelson drives the point home in "Dred Scott's Case—Reconsidered," December, 1953), because Congress was desperate to shrug off the responsibility, it gave the Court the legislative go-ahead to save the nation. In 1848, the Clayton compromise bill tied to the scheme of congressional noninterference the additional principle that the question of slavery in the territories should rest on the Constitution as expounded by the territorial courts, with the right of appeal to the Supreme Court. This bill passed the Senate but failed in the House; the principle of a judicial solution, however, was incorporated in 1850 into the bills organizing the territories of Utah and New Mexico and in the Kansas-Nebraska Act of 1854. Desirous of smashing radicalism, made confident by past success, encouraged by presidential and congressional importuning, the Court took up the Constitution and set off to rescue the fortunes of the Union.

Though the Court was damned for acting, it would just as surely have been damned for doing nothing. Perhaps, then, the real tragedy was the way the Court acted. It is tantalizing to speculate on the results of an opinion upholding Congress' power over slavery in the territories. Such a decision would have been consistent both with practice and with the Court's often-stated rule that it was guided by well-established usage. Popular sovereignty as a compromise solution would then have become constitutionally feasible. To be sure, the Northern Democrats in 1860 would have had to accept the 1854 repeal of the Missouri Compromise, but, with the prospect of a free Kansas, they might have done so. And without the *Dred Scott* rule to fall back on, it is possible that the South would have settled for popular sovereignty as the best available alternative. The Democratic party, the potential vehicle for compromise, might then have held together. Congress would have been given back the responsibility it had passed on so unchivalrously. The Court could have escaped the devastating burden, which *Dred Scott* placed on it, of opposing the moral majority of the nation. It might be insisted, of course, as Taney himself did insist, that his statement on slavery and Negro rights was true to the document of 1787. Sad to say it was. But if there was any controlling principle of constitutional law established during the age of

Marshall and Taney, it was that the Constitution of 1787 must and could change to meet the various crises of the American people. Slavery in 1857 was a new crisis.

So much for the "if's." Once in the breach, the Court's course of action was predictable. As John R. Schmidhauser shows in "Judicial Behavior and the Sectional Crisis" (November, 1961), the background influence of party and section were never absent from decision-making in the Taney Court. (Schmidhauser's scalogram analysis of decisions on the sectionally sensitive issues of commerce, corporations, and slavery makes the point conclusively and conveniently rates the justices from 1837–60 according to their varying susceptibility to party preferences and regional views of social and economic issues.) Such influences were frequently not controlling, rarely gross; but in a subtle way they influenced the outlook and thus the opinions of the judges. Considering that seven of the nine justices, all of those who sided with Taney, were Democrats, it is not astonishing that the *Dred Scott* decision fit neatly into the Jacksonian scheme. It negated federal power in fact—by denying Congress authority to prohibit slavery in the territories —and preserved it in theory—by conceding Congress the power and responsibility to protect slavery there. Congressional authority over commerce, banking, and internal improvements had been curtailed when such action threatened state or sectional interests. Why not curtail it over slavery? The Court protected the property interests of corporate capitalism; should not its guardianship embrace the property interests of Southern agrarian capitalism as well? In answering these questions— questions which could affect the fate of Southern civilization so markedly—time-engrained values and sentiments could not be suppressed. The "five Southerners and two doughfaces" did not conspire; they succumbed.

THE WAR YEARS: THE COURT SURVIVES

Fought to preserve the Constitution, the war in fact laid siege to it. The magnitude and unprecedented nature of that crisis called forth a flood of decisions that went beyond the regular channels of constitutional law and swept over the classic constitutional barriers against governmental abuse of power. An effective two-party system faded into Republican dominance, though it remained theoretically alive. Separation of powers gave way, in fact if not theory, as wartime decision-making shifted to the President. The delicate balance between state and federal powers which the Court had labored to establish was permanently disrupted as the federal government consolidated the duties—military, financial, and administrative—which the states could not perform. The necessities of war took priority over individual freedom and private property. Order and the rule of law grappled feebly with chaos and expediency.

The Civil War reminds us, as it must have the judges themselves, that the Court shares the lawmaking process with the other branches and with the people and that its power varies with historical circumstances. The Court functions most effectively in periods demanding and permitting moderate adjustments in the constitutional system. As Arthur Bestor put it so well, during the Civil War "the question of how the Constitution ought to operate as a piece of working machinery was superseded by the question of whether it might and should be dismantled." Even if the Court had been popular, vital, and united—and at this time the Taney Court was none of these—it would have been hard pressed to maintain constitutional integrity against what a morally aroused populace and a determined Congress and President decided was military necessity. With the Republican victory in 1860, the Court confronted a party whose platform of opposition to slavery in the territories directly challenged the *Dred Scott* decision. With the secession of the Southern states, the Court presided over a nation which condemned it. Powerful anti-Court forces in and out of Congress cried for retribution. Some demanded the repeal of Section 25 of the Judiciary Act of 1789, some wanted to pack the Court to make it representative, and others would abolish it and start from scratch. And besides all this, the Court was very weak within. The frequent illnesses of Catron, Grier, Wayne, and Taney greatly reduced efficiency and vitality. Institutional continuity was disrupted by deaths, resignations, and the creation of a new judicial circuit—which meant that six new justices were appointed between 1857 and 1864. In short, it was not just a question of whether the Court could save the Constitution but whether it could save itself.

The Court survived at the price of personal and doctrinal "Republicanization." Fortunately, Lincoln and his party were more interested in dominating the Court than in destroying it, and they were soon successful. By 1862, the President had appointed three justices of acceptable political persuasion, and two more by 1865, including an abolitionist Chief Justice. And by then, Congress had reorganized judicial circuits giving preponderance to the North. But even before these changes, the Court did nothing to challenge seriously the President's wartime manipulation of the Constitution. To be sure, the old Chief Justice spoke out valiantly. In Baltimore, under martial law enforced by Union troops, he delivered his circuit opinion in *Ex parte Merryman* (1861), defending judicial over martial law and condemning the presidential suspension of the privilege of the writ of habeas corpus as an unconstitutional usurpation of congressional power. Taney audaciously sent a copy to President Lincoln, but his ruling was just ignored. Though the *Merryman* case never came before the Supreme Court, in *Ex parte Vallandigham* (1864), the Court had a chance to rule on the constitutionality of military rule in an area where the civil courts were active, but it begged off on jurisdictional grounds. The Chief Justice remained undaunted; he was prepared to strike down the Legal Tender Act (a wartime measure which made government notes legal tender for all public and private debts), national conscription, and the emancipation of the slaves if these questions came before the Court—but they never did.

Only once, in the *Prize Cases* of 1863, did the Court directly confront constitutional issues raised by the war. Here it showed its dexterity in making certain that necessity found a law. The questions raised by the *Prize Cases* were of a fundamental nature. The first was whether the President had the power to proclaim a blockade in the absence of a congressional declaration of war. The Court sanctioned executive action, arguing that a state of war already existed even though it had not been recognized by Congress; in effect, the President had merely responded to the grim reality. Having acknowledged the existence of a state of war, the Court was then faced with the thorny problem of defining its legal nature, i.e., whether it was a conflict between nations or an insurrection or rebellion by private persons against a legal government. Recognition of the full belligerent status of the Confederacy would acknowledge the legality of secession, invite foreign countries to recognize the Southern nation, and tie the hands of the administration in dealing with Southern persons and property. To define the clash as an insurrection would avoid these dangers and actually strengthen the powers of the executive in meeting the emergency. But the blockade was an act of war inferring belligerency, and there were advantages, regarding prisoners and other matters, in extending a qualified belligerent status to the South. By assuming that the conflict was a war and at the same time an insurrection, the Court let the administration have it both ways. The job of determining when it was which was left to the political departments, and the Court was willing to accept their decisions as binding.

Filled with Republican justices, headed by an abolitionist, and responsive to the requirements of the war effort, the Court recovered popularity and prestige. Cooperating with the executive and Congress on Reconstruction came naturally, and, by the 1870's, the Court was ready to launch out on a remarkable spree of judicial activism, if not usurpation. Though the Court survived, it did little during the war to keep alive the axiom of constitutional government—law, and not men, rule. That the rule of law was maintained at all, J. H. Randall concluded in his *Constitutional Problems Under Lincoln* (1964), was due more to Lincoln's respect for the Constitution (even while he was straining it) and to the "American people's sense of constitutional government," than to the efforts of the Court. Yet it must be added that the people's "fundamental sense of respect" for constitutionalism owed much to the dedicated and educative statesmanship which the Marshall and Taney Courts displayed for over sixty years.

Is there any better plan, whatever imperfections our present one may have, for securing a reasonably continuous, non-partisan and philosophical exposition of the Constitution than by regarding it as the supreme law of the land to be applied in actual cases and controversies through the exercise of judicial power?

CHARLES EVANS HUGHES (1928)

S I X

The Legacy of the Supreme Court under Marshall and Taney

History is a stern judge. By its standard, past accomplishments are rated according to their relevance to the changing present. Such has been the case with the Marshall and Taney Courts. Each Court had a distinct constitutional character, a style of its own; each has faced the test of historical relevancy on its unique merits.

For the Marshall Court there has been no problem. It worked for a powerful, self-sufficient, centralized nation resting on an economic foundation of commerce and free enterprise; democracy was left to fend for itself. To achieve its goals the Marshall Court enlarged and consolidated national power and put it at the service of expanding capitalism. Without doubt, American history has favored the principles Marshall worked for. Power, and with it responsibility, have moved inexorably from the local and state levels to the nation; the nation itself has risen to the pinnacle of world power. The multi-cultural heritage is fast dissolving in the American melting-pot and, increasingly, the various notions of the good life have given way to a standardized American Dream. Commerce and enterprise have been the basis of national greatness and the substance of the dream. Because it was unequivocally committed to nationalism and capitalism and was instrumental in the development of both, the Marshall Court has retained its relevance in American history and held a favored place in American historiography. Critics of big business and big government, of course, have found less to extol. But even the reformers have been hard pressed to make an effective case against the Marshall Court, because—at least since Woodrow Wilson—they too have relied on the power of the federal government to implement their programs. Though Jefferson is their hero, Marshall has proved historically indispensable.

History and historians have not treated the Taney Court so well. First, there is the problem of slavery. It may be true that the views of the members of the Taney Court did not differ greatly from those of Marshall and his colleagues on this subject, that the Taney Court did not conspire with Southern slaveholders, and further that what it did to the Negro was no worse than what subsequent generations of Americans were to do. Yet, the fact remains that the Court did choose—from several alternatives and against the will of the majority—to bolster the cause of slavery. However slowly and painfully, American history has been moving toward meaningful freedom for the Negro; understanding the Taney Court's dilemma cannot put it on the winning side of this struggle.

But if the Taney Court was reactionary, it was also (as Robert J. Harris reminds us in "Chief Justice Taney: Prophet of Reform and Reaction," February, 1957) forward-looking and reform-minded. It did not challenge capitalism and nationalism head on. But, taking its cue from Jacksonian democracy, it sensed the threat to democracy from corporate interests in league with government. It appreciated the democratic nature of state legislatures and invited them to regulate the new economic forces in the interest of the public and for the benefit of the common man. In doing so, the Taney Court faced up to the growing maturity and importance of legislative government and the corresponding need to impose realistic limits on judicial policy-making. It is not likely that some future revival of Jacksonian states' rights sentiment will carry the Taney Court to historiographical glory. But it is conceivable that a realization of the diminishing efficiency of national power and its threat to individual freedom will lead historians to appreciate the concepts the Taney Court stood for—cultural pluralism, local responsibility, and suspicion of power.

So much for historical evaluation based on the separate and distinct accomplishments of the Marshall and Taney Courts. Such an approach, given the real differences in the Courts, has its place. But the Marshall and Taney Courts were really more alike than different. They contributed jointly to the continuous development of the Supreme Court as an institution of government. Together they laid the foundation of American jurisprudence. Both influenced and were influenced by the same fundamental assumptions of American culture. Finally, then, one is obliged to turn from the Marshall and Taney Courts to the Supreme Court under Marshall and Taney.

The symbiotic relationship between law and social change (described generally in Willard Hurst's *Law and Social Process in United States History,* 1960) was especially productive in the age of Marshall and Taney. During these formative years basic propositions of national culture took shape and were given legal form. Property was identified with liberty. Material progress became the measure of individual merit and national greatness. And the corollary principle—that government should serve both individual and national progress by aiding capitalism —was established as well. The Supreme Court did not create these social axioms, but neither did it merely reflect them. The court room was a forum where Americans debated conflicting interests. And when the highest court in the land decided cases, it put the collective authority of the people behind one set of interests and gave priority to the social values on which they rested. In the process of resolving the controversies of Americans over a period of sixty-four years, the Supreme Court formulated the legal principles and the intellectual justification for the free enterprise system. It facilitated the transition from the unified corporate society of the eighteenth century to the atomistic one of the twentieth—the transition, in Sir Henry Maine's classic phrase, "from status to contract." Far from being overwhelmed by this cultural transformation, the Court presided over it.

In laying the legal foundation for free enterprise, the Court under Marshall and Taney proved itself to be a representative institution in the broad sense. One hastens to add that it did not represent all Americans. Capitalism Horatio Alger style meant little to the piece-worker of Philadelphia, who labored fourteen hours a day for as many cents, or to the women and children in the Northern factories, or to millions of black Americans. Then as now, the law was often irrelevant for these anonymous poor, and they aspired outside and often against it. The futility of their aspirations presents a vital corrective to the myth of the "happy republic." The legal principles of capitalism, however, made sense to the dominant power groups and to the large middle class of Americans, who also shared in American affluence. For this class, which aspired to move ahead without losing what it already had, a constitutional system that permitted change and yet ordered it and kept it in trustworthy hands was appropriate. De Tocqueville missed the point when he pitted judicial government against majoritarian democracy. The Court may have restrained the majority by forcing it to justify its means and ends in terms of law. But far from opposing majority will, the Court finally served it. Because it did, the American democrat was willing to talk the language of law and order and be educated to the virtues of conservative change. By educating so well, the Court, to no small degree, made constitutional conservatism the other face of majoritarian liberalism.

Whether the doctrine of law and order and the legal principles fashioned to serve free enterprise in the heroic age continue to be entirely relevant today is another question. The basic assumptions that property and liberty are identical and that freedom means free enterprise do not mean very much in an age when property is often a quarterly dividend rather than the extension of one's creative self, and they have no meaning at all to the millions with no real stake in society. It cannot be said that law and order—which the early Court did so much to institutionalize—has become irrelevant. But that principle is not self-sufficient and it has not insured social justice. Frequently, it has been invoked to prevent necessary reform rather than to check reckless change. In other words, law is not synonymous with morality. If it did nothing else, *Dred Scott* showed that the two are sometimes distinct, even unequal. It was not due process of law, but the holocaust of civil war which freed the slaves. And radicalism continued to be the incitement to social reform in America, even though the reforms were finally embodied in law. The Court's contributions to law and order can be justly praised, but it must not be forgotten that the political process in America has relied and continues to rely for vitality on extra-legal, sometimes illegal, radicalism.

Yet, because some of the assumptions formulated for an earlier age are no longer entirely applicable to the needs of modern America, this does not mean that the legacy of the early Court is irrelevant. The truly great achievement of the Court under Marshall and Taney is that in formulating legal principles for its time, it refused to stamp them with categorical finality. The Court accepted without question the cultural assumptions of the age. But it also saw that change was the essence of the American experience and it accommodated the Constitution to this central fact. Because it did, the Court survived its mistakes and shortcomings. In surviving it left a vital institutional legacy: established judicial procedures, tried and proven techniques of judicial statecraft, nascent judicial self-consciousness, and a tradition of pragmatic responsiveness to the facts of American life. When the modern Court has reacted to social crises in the twentieth century, as it did after 1937 when it stopped trying to regulate the economy and took on the task of protecting individual liberty from government power, it has built on the foundation laid by the early Court.

In short, constitutional law under Marshall and Taney was a victory of process over substance. The victory was embodied in a vital, organic Constitution capable of ordering, yet responsive to, historical change. The method was amendment by judicial review. The system was adumbrated by the Framers of the Constitution, implemented and amplified by the Marshall Court, and tested and verified by the Taney Court. In reply to Charles Evans Hughes' question, it is a constitutional system which the American people have accepted as the best they can get.

Bibliography

Constitutional law begins with the Constitution, and an understanding of that document in its historical context is the indispensable foundation for further study. An account of the deliberations of the Framers—and an informative introduction as well—is in Max Farrand (ed.), *The Records of the Federal Convention of 1787* (4 vols., 1911, 1937) and an account of the state ratifying conventions is in Jonathan Elliott, *The Debates in the Several State Conventions on the Adoption of the Federal Constitution* (5 vols., 1836). Unexcelled for its detailed yet readable exegesis of the Constitution is *The Constitution of the United States of America:*

Analysis and Interpretation (1953), prepared by the Legislative Reference Service of the Library of Congress under the editorship of Edward S. Corwin. And Corwin's *The "Higher Law" Background of American Constitutional Law* (1959), reprinted from his earlier articles in the *Harvard Law Review,* is outstanding on the intellectual background of the Constitution. For highlights of the historiographical debate over the immediate historical forces which shaped the Constitution, see Charles Beard's *An Economic Interpretation of the Constitution* (1913), Forrest McDonald's *We the People: The Economic Origins of the Constitution* (1958) and his *E Pluribus Unum: The Formation of the American Republic 1776–1790* (1965). To balance McDonald, there is Lee Benson, *Turner and Beard: American Historical Writing Reconsidered* (1960), J. T. Main, *The Anti-Federalists: Critics of the Constitution, 1781–1788* (1962), Staughton Lynd, *Class Conflict, Slavery, and the United States Constitution* (1967), and Stanley Elkins and Eric McKitrick, "The Founding Fathers: Young Men of the Republic," 76 *Political Science Quarterly* (No. 2, 1961).

Regarding the Court's role in the constitutional establishment, there is no substitute for reading both Article III, Sections 1 and 2, of the Constitution and the Federal Judiciary Act of 1789 (1 Statutes at Large 73) in conjunction with Charles Warren, "New Light on the History of the Federal Judiciary Act of 1789," 37 *Harvard Law Review* (November, 1923). The changing organization, jurisdiction, and practice of the Court is analyzed in Felix Frankfurter and J. M. Landis, *The Business of the Supreme Court* (1928), and in Homer Cummings and Carl McFarland, *Federal Justice* (1937). These accounts are supplemented by Curtis P. Nettels' analysis of how politics and sectionalism shaped the structure of the federal courts in "The Mississippi Valley and the Federal Judiciary, 1807–37," 12 *Mississippi Valley Historical Review* (September, 1925).

The foundation blocks of all scholarship on the Court are, of course, the opinions of the judges. Although it is good strategy to consult a general account of the Court first, the serious student will want to go directly to the Supreme Court Reports. The first ninety volumes (through 1874) are cited according to the name of the "official" reporter: thus 4 Peters 514 (1830) refers to volume 4 of Peters' reports at page 514 for 1830. Various unofficial editions of the *United States Reports* (the *Lawyers' Edition* is the standard one) are "star paged" (e.g., *514) to indicate pages in the original reports. The most complete and accessible collection of federal circuit and district court decisions before 1880 (though only a few of the latter are extant) is the thirty-volume series called *Federal Cases.* Leading opinions are available in a number of recent collections such as those of R. E. Cushing, W. F. Dodd, L. B. Evans, and Charles Fairman. James B. Thayer's *Cases on Constitutional Law* (2 vols., 1895) remains the outstanding annotated collection of cases for the nineteenth century. *Liberty and Justice* (1963), edited by James M. Smith and Paul Murphy, includes not only leading cases but related constitutional documents as well. As a guide to research in the reports and other basic legal materials, consult Miles O. Price and Harry Bitner, *Effective Legal Research* (1953).

A wide variety of materials useful in reconstructing the legal atmosphere in which the antebellum Court operated is now available. The first American law periodical (Hall's *American Law Journal*) appeared in 1808 and, by the end of the Marshall period, several more (the *American Jurist and Law Magazine* being the most broad-based and inquiring) had appeared with a notable advance in coverage and sophistication. Complete runs of these revealing journals are now available in the "American Periodical Series, 1800–1850" (University Microfilms). The cultural drive for a national jurisprudence, especially during the ebullient period after 1815, also prompted a spate of commentaries on American law. All insisted (even the most common-law oriented) that the American experience demanded a unique American law, but they disagreed over nationalism and states' rights. Works of St. George Tucker, his son Henry, and John Taylor of Caroline County argued the latter case, while Justice Joseph Story produced the most distinguished nationalist exposition (*Commentaries on the Constitution of the United States,* 3 vols., 1833). Rising above all others in scholarship and permanent value, however, was Chancellor James Kent's *Commentaries on American Law* (4 vols., 1826–30; see especially Oliver Wendell Holmes' definitive 12th edition). Perry Miller's edition of the writings of these and other contemporaries in *The Legal Mind in America* (1962) and Charles Haar's superb collection of essays, letters, and speeches in *The Golden Age of American Law* (1965) provides ready access to the central legal ideas of the formative period—and dispels the notion that American legal thought began with Oliver Wendell Holmes.

THE SUPREME COURT AND THE JUDICIAL PROCESS

Before plunging into the primary sources or the labyrinth of general and specialized historiography of the Court, some knowledge of the judicial function—and hopefully a feeling for the men who perform it—is desirable. The writings of great justices provide an interesting and useful place to begin. Max Lerner's *The Mind and Faith of Justice Holmes* (1943) brings together many of the deep insights into the judicial process of that distinguished judge. Chief Justice Charles Evans Hughes' *The Supreme Court of the United States* (1928) mixes the functional and historical approach and is informed by learning and experience. Benjamin Cardozo's *The Nature of the Judicial Process* (1921) remains a classic analysis of the ingredients of decision-making. Justice Robert Jackson's *The Supreme Court in the American System of Government* (1955) is a more practical-minded treatment of the Court's position in the governmental process. Few have written on the judicial process with such insight and grace as Justice Felix Frankfurter: recommended are the various essays in *Law and Politics* (1939), *Of Law and Men* (1956), *Felix Frankfurter Reminisces* (1960), and *Of Law and Life and Other Things that Matter* (1965). Finally, Alan Westin's *An Autobiography of the Supreme Court* (1963) is a unique selection of "off-the-bench" commentary by Supreme Court Justices from Jay to Warren.

Among the many studies of the institutional and functional nature of the Court by non-judges, the following are noteworthy: James B. Thayer, "The Origin and Scope of the American Doctrine of Constitutional Law," 7 *Harvard Law Review* (October, 1893); K. N. Llewellyn, "The Constitution as an Institution," 34 *Columbia Law Review* (January, 1934); Thomas R. Powell, "The Logic and Rhetoric of Constitutional Law," 15 *Journal of Philosophy, Psychology and Scientific Method* (November, 1918); Robert A. Dahl, "Decision-Making in a Democracy: The Supreme Court as a National Policy-Maker," 6 *Journal of Public Law* (No. 2, 1957); Alpheus T. Mason, "The Supreme Court: Temple and Forum," 48 *Yale Law Review* (Summer, 1959). Max Lerner broadens the picture in "Constitution and Court as Symbols," 46 *Yale Law Journal* (June, 1937) by putting the Court in the context of intellectual history. Also concerned with seeing the Court in the larger sweep is Eugene V. Rostow, "The Democratic Character of Judicial Review," 66 *Harvard Law Review* (December, 1952). Some of these and a wealth of other essays and cases illustrating the "functioning of the judiciary in the context of the American political process" are found in the excellent compilation, *Courts, Judges and Politics* (1961), edited by Walter F. Murphy and C. Herman Pritchett. In *The Supreme Court: Law and Discretion* (1967), Wallace Mendelson brings together conflicting views—from both on and off the bench—on the classic issue of judicial activism. Thomas Reed Powell's *Vagaries and Varieties in Constitutional Interpretation* (1956) contains the unusually acute observations of a distinguished teacher and scholar. Complementary aspects of the judicial process are treated in Edward H. Levi, *An Introduction to Legal Reasoning* (1948), which analyzes the internal logic of decision-making and Walter F. Murphy, *Elements of Judicial Strategy* (1964), which puts judicial decisions in the larger strategic perspective.

GENERAL HISTORIES OF THE SUPREME COURT

Regardless of its pro-Court bias, the prodigious scholarship of Charles Warren's *The Supreme Court in United States History* (2 vols., 1937) makes it the outstanding general history of the Court. Highly critical of the Court, on the other hand, are Gustavus Myers' socialist *History of the Supreme Court* (1912) and Louis Boudin's *Government by Judiciary* (2 vols., 1932). Boudin sets out to demonstrate that, from the start, judicial power has encroached on the "legitimate rights of legislature, executive and people"; though massive in its scholarship, this work is marred by excessive special pleading. Not until the publication of Charles Grove Haines' *The Role of the Supreme Court in American Government and Politics 1789–1835* (1944) and the companion volume by Haines and Foster H. Sherwood (1957), covering the period from 1835 to 1864, was there a comprehensive answer to Warren's pro-Court, nationalist interpretation. William W. Crosskey, in *Politics and the Constitution in the History of the United States* (2 vols., 1953), attempted to swing the interpretive pendulum back by arguing that the Constitution established a unitary government, but his provocative argument has left most scholars unconvinced. Though not exactly a comprehensive history, *Selected Essays in Constitutional Law* (4 vols., 1938), compiled by the Association of American Law Schools, is richly informative.

Among the several constitutional histories that discuss Congress and the executive as well as the Court, three are notable: Andrew C. McLaughlin, *A Constitutional History of the United States* (1935) led the way and, though in need of revision, it still merits attention. Carl B. Swisher's *American Constitutional Development* (2nd ed., 1954) is distinguished by its incisive scholarship and shares current popularity with Alfred H. Kelly and Winfred A. Harbison, *The American Constitution* (3rd ed., 1963). The latter is outstanding for its comprehensiveness and thorough historical background. Among the more streamlined histories that focus entirely on the Court, Benjamin F. Wright's *The Growth of American Constitutional Law* (1942) is still read for its clarity and interpretive excellence. Fred Rodell, *Nine Men* (1964 ed.) and Robert G. McCloskey, *The American Supreme Court* (1960) stand out among the more recent short histories. The former is acknowledgedly an "oh-hell-I-might-as-well-do-it-myself" book but beneath the crusty style are some deep insights into judicial history. McCloskey's graceful and balanced book is perhaps the best short history of the whole Court now available.

No discussion of general scholarship on the Court would be complete without special mention of Edward S. Corwin. With a mastery of institutional history and legal and political philosophy, he combined hard-nosed judicial realism and a dedication to historical truth. Corwin's great synthetical work was never written, but in some twenty monographs and countless articles and reviews he supplied the germinal ideas which enriched the whole field of constitutional literature. The best of his essays, collected by Alpheus T. Mason and Gerald Garvey in *American Constitutional History: Essays by Edward S. Corwin* (1964) reads like an interpretive history of the Court.

THE CLOSE VIEW: MONOGRAPHS AND ARTICLES ON THE MARSHALL AND TANEY COURTS

Some of the most useful scholarship is that which deals with special themes or phases of the Court's work. Frankfurter's *The Commerce Clause under Marshall, Taney, and Waite* (1937), for example, gives a consecutive interpretation of that crucial phase of the Court's work which cannot be found in general accounts. In *The Contract Clause of the Constitution* (1938), Benjamin F. Wright does the same for that subject. John R. Schmidhauser singles out a vital function of judicial history for special treatment in *The Supreme Court as Final Arbiter in Federal-State Relations, 1789–1957* (1958). Mitchell Wendell, *Relations between the Federal and State Courts* (1949) deals with another aspect—and a seriously neglected one—of the federal-state relationship.

The impact of constitutional law on the economic process is another subject which has received much profitable attention. The Court's role in bringing the Constitution to the service of private property is the subject of Corwin's classic essay, "The Basic Doctrine of American Constitutional Law," 12 *Michigan Law Review* (February, 1914). Max Lerner's "Supreme Court and American Capitalism," 42 *Yale Law Journal* (March, 1933) puts the Court's economic role in the cultural setting. A more detailed treatment of the same general subject is Howard J. Graham's "Procedure to Substance—Extra-Judicial Rise of Due Process, 1830–1860," 40 *California Law Review* (Winter, 1952–53). Wallace Mendelson's *Capitalism, Democracy, and the Supreme Court* (1960) relates the capitalistic tendencies of American law to democratic political development and uses this economic touchstone to distinguish the Taney from the Marshall Court.

No legal development in the formative period has had more impact on American history than the rise of the corporation, and on that subject E. M. Dodd's *American Business Corporations until 1860* (1954) is indispensable. The historical background not supplied by Dodd can be obtained in John P. Davis, *Corporations: A Study of the Origin and Development of Great Business Combinations and Their Relation to the Authority of the State* (2 vols., 1905; Capricorn Books, 1961) and Joseph S. Davis, *Essays in the Earlier History of American Corporations* (2 vols., 1917). Very useful on selected aspects of corporate development are: Oscar and Mary Handlin, "Origins of the American Business Corporation," 5 *Journal of Economic History* (May, 1945), G. S. Callender, "The Early Transportation and Banking Enterprises of the States in Relation to the Growth of Corporations," 17 *Quarterly Journal of Economics* (November, 1902), and Gerald C. Henderson, *The Position of Foreign Corporations in American Constitutional Law* (1918).

Useful in adding refinement to the legal picture of the Marshall-Taney period are those accounts which treat in depth particular decisions or special aspects of the Court's history. Clarification of two major episodes concerning the early political battles of the Marshall Court can be found in Kathryn Turner, "Federalist Policy and the Judicial Act of 1801," 22 *William and Mary Quarterly* (January, 1965) and Richard B. Lillich, "The Chase Impeachment," 4 *American Journal of Legal History* (January, 1960). Robert K. Faulkner's "John Marshall and the Burr Trial," 53 *Journal of American History* (September, 1966) effectively revises the old allegation of Corwin and others that Marshall's hatred of Jefferson influenced his doctrine of treason in the Burr trial. Kenneth Treacy, "The Olmstead Case, 1778–1809," *Western Political Quarterly* (September, 1957) traces the complex history of the Court's prolonged and finally successful effort to impress its legal will on a recalcitrant state. Paul Gates' "Tenants of the Log Cabin," 49 *Mississippi Valley Historical Review* (June, 1962) analyzes the Court's failure to do so in *Green* v. *Biddle*. Both articles supply a valuable corrective to the notion that constitutional history begins and ends with judicial decisions. Another valuable work which treats the political and economic setting of an important decision fully is C. P. Magrath, *Yazoo: Law and Politics in the New Republic: The Case of* Fletcher *v.* Peck (1966).

Three somewhat broader interpretive articles on the Marshall period are notable because they succeed in destroying the myth of a unitary, Marshall-dominated Court. Donald Morgan traces the rise of internal division on the Court in "The Origin of Supreme Court Dissent," 10 *William and Mary Quarterly* (July, 1953). Donald Roper's excellent article, "Judicial Unanimity and the Marshall Court—A Road to Reappraisal," 9 *American Journal of Legal History* (April, 1965) expands Morgan's thesis by noting the composite, often compromising, nature of many key decisions of the Marshall Court. Gerald Garvey, "The Constitutional Revolution of 1837 and the Myth of Marshall's Monolith," 18 *Western Political Quarterly* (March, 1965) makes a similar point and shows how the doctrinal flexibility of the Marshall Court left the Taney Court decisional elbowroom that permitted a nonrevolutionary accommodation of old law to new history.

For the Taney period, Richard Longaker's "Andrew Jackson and the Judiciary," 71 *Political Science Quarterly* (September,

1956), makes a valuable contribution by correcting the misconception that President Jackson was implacably hostile to the judiciary and the law. Curtis P. Nettels' above-mentioned "Mississippi Valley and the Federal Judiciary" amplifies this revision by noting that the West wanted more federal courts, not fewer. On the general relationship of judicial power and political parties, Stuart Nagel's "Political Parties and Judicial Review in American History," 11 *Journal of Public Law* (No. 2, 1962) is provocative, though not focused on the antebellum period.

Much of the specialized literature on the Taney Court deals with the slavery-sectional controversy. In this category Staughton Lynd, "The Compromise of 1787," 81 *Political Science Quarterly* (June, 1966) starts at the beginning by going beyond the sparse documents of the constitutional period to hypothesize on the nature of the 1787 compromise on slavery. His "Abolitionist Critique of the United States Constitution," in Martin Duberman (ed.), *The Antislavery Vanguard* (1965), points up the continued influence of the sectional mind on constitutional interpretation. These essays can now be found in Lynd's previously mentioned *Class Conflict, Slavery, and the United States Constitution.* As a background to the Court's involvement in the constitutional debate over slavery in the territories, two articles by Arthur Bestor are superb: "State Sovereignty and Slavery: A Reinterpretation of Proslavery Constitutional Doctrine, 1846–1860," 54 *Journal of the Illinois State Historical Society* (Summer, 1961) and "The American Civil War as a Constitutional Crisis," 69 *American Historical Review* (January, 1964).

John R. Schmidhauser, "Judicial Behavior and the Sectional Crisis of 1837–1860," 23 *Journal of Politics* (November, 1961) uses statistical techniques to establish the vulnerability of the justices to sectional issues, including slavery. The standard compilation of slavery cases is Helen T. Catterall, *Judicial Cases Concerning American Slavery and the Negro* (5 vols., 1937). John C. Hurd, *The Law of Freedom and Bondage in the United States* (2 vols., 1858–62) is still useful for understanding the complex legal structure which sustained slavery. On one crucial facet of that structure, Allen Johnson's "Constitutionality of the Fugitive Slave Acts," 31 *Yale Law Journal* (December, 1920) remains the standard account. J. L. Nogee's "Prigg Case and Fugitive Slavery, 1842–1850," 39 *Journal of Negro History* (July, 1954) throws light on that crucial case as do both William Leslie's

"The Influence of Joseph Story's Theory of the Conflict of Laws on Constitutional Nationalism," 35 *Mississippi Valley Historical Review* (September, 1948) and Joseph C. Burke's "What Did the Prigg Decision Really Decide?" 93 *Pennsylvania Magazine of History and Biography* (January, 1969). In "Some Antecedents of the Dred Scott Case," 30 *American Historical Review* (October, 1924), Helen T. Catterall traces the decisions that, she contends, led inevitably to *Dred Scott*. Wallace Mendelson, in "Dred Scott's Case—Reconsidered," 38 *Minnesota Law Review* (December, 1953), shows how Congress helped the Court on its way to that disaster.

On the *Dred Scott* decision itself the literature is abundant and contradictory. But thanks to Frederick S. Allis, Jr., "The Dred Scott Labyrinth," in H. Stuart Hughes (ed.), *Teachers of History: Essays in Honor of Laurence Bradford Packard* (1954), it need not be overwhelming. Vincent S. Hopkins's *Dred Scott's Case* (1951) is the most complete discussion of complex legal aspects of the case. On the controversial question of what was before the Court, Edward S. Corwin, "The Dred Scott Decision in the Light of Contemporary Legal Doctrines," 17 *American Historical Review* (October, 1911) and Horace H. Hagan, "The Dred Scott Decision," 15 *Georgetown Law Journal* (January, 1926) argue persuasively for the technical correctness of Taney's decision to canvass the whole issue. On that point, however, Frank H. Hodder, "Some Phases of the Dred Scott Case," 16 *Mississippi Valley Historical Review* (June, 1929) and Richard R. Stenberg, "Some Political Aspects of the Dred Scott Case," 19 *Mississippi Valley Historical Review* (March, 1933) remain unconvinced. Additional bibliography on the opinion and a nice selection of contemporary and current views of its meaning can be found in Stanley Kutler (ed.), *The Dred Scott Decision: Law or Politics?* (1967).

On the Court during the Civil War, one can consult David M. Silver, *Lincoln's Supreme Court* (1956) and especially J. G. Randall's *Constitutional Problems under Lincoln* (rev. ed., 1964).

JUDICIAL BIOGRAPHY

This genre (J. W. Peltason's "Supreme Court Biography and the Study of Public Law," in Gottfried Dietze, ed., *Essays on the American Constitution* [1964] discusses the matter with insight) performs a variety of historiographical functions. Above all, however, it can illuminate the relationship of human experience and character to decision-making and, by treating the Court from the inside, supply a realistic dimension lacking in institutional history.

Albert Beveridge, *The Life of John Marshall* (4 vols., 1916–1919), regardless of its conservative-nationalist bias and excessively heroic view of Marshall, is still the standard biography of the great Chief Justice. And the third and fourth volumes constitute, in fact, an indispensable general history of the Marshall Court. Though not a full biography, Edward S. Corwin, *John Marshall and the Constitution* (1919) merits reading. W. Melville Jones (ed.), *Chief Justice John Marshall: A Reappraisal* (1956) contains a valuable collection of essays on Marshall by distinguished scholars. The most exhaustive and analytical study of the Chief Justice's legal position is Robert K. Faulkner, *The Jurisprudence of John Marshall* (1968). In "Mr. Chief Justice Marshall," in Allison Dunham and Philip B. Kurland, *Mr. Justice* (rev. ed., 1964), William Crosskey presents the provocative thesis (which finds some support in the previously cited articles of Roper and Garvey) that Marshall compromised true national principles of constitutional law to accommodate the Republican philosophy of his colleagues on the bench. Among those accounts which take Marshall off the pedestal and put him back in history, Max Lerner's "John Marshall and the Campaign of History," 39 *Columbia Law Review* (March, 1939), is outstanding. Justice Frankfurter, "John Marshall and the Judicial Function," 69 *Harvard Law Review* (December, 1955), effectively relates the Chief Justice to American constitutional history. On the remarkable intellectual relationship between the two giants of American constitutional development, read Samuel Konefsky, *John Marshall and Alexander Hamilton: Architects of the American Constitution* (1964). And on the not-so-friendly but historically significant relationship between Marshall and Jefferson, see Julian P. Boyd, "The Chasm that Separated Thomas Jefferson and John Marshall," in G. Dietze (ed.), *Essays on the American Constitution* (1964). Another of the Chief Justice's most articulate enemies is given his intellectual due in the anonymous note, "Judge Spencer Roane of Virginia—Champion of States' Rights—Foe of John Marshall," 66 *Harvard Law Review* (May, 1953). For still other material on Marshall, see James A. Servies, *A Bibliography of John Marshall* (1956). Despite this voluminous literature, however, a balanced and up-to-date biography of Marshall is much needed; hopefully the definitive edition of the Marshall Papers now underway (under the editorship of Stephen Kurtz) will lead to one.

Marshall's most distinguished colleague, Justice Joseph Story, also deserves fuller attention. Until the completion of the biographies now in progress, generally reliable information can be found in W. W. Story (ed.), *The Life and Letters of Joseph Story* (2 vols., 1852). Henry Steele Commager, "Joseph Story," in *The Gasper G. Bacon Lectures on the Constitution of the United States, 1940–1950* (1953) is a very readable summary of Story's public career. For more particular aspects of Story's life see Gerald Dunne's "Joseph Story: The Germinal Years," "Joseph Story: 1812 Overture," "Joseph Story: The Great Term," "Joseph Story: The Middle Years," in *Harvard Law Review*, 75 (February, 1962), 77 (December, 1963), 79 (March, 1966), 80 (June, 1967); Morgan Dowd, "Justice Story: A Study of the Legal Philosophy of a Jeffersonian Judge," 18 *Vanderbilt Law Review* (March, 1965); and R. Kent Newmyer, "A Note on the Whig Politics of Justice Joseph Story," 48 *Mississippi Valley Historical Review* (December, 1961), as well as his "Joseph Story and the War of 1812: A Judicial Nationalist," 26 *The Historian* (August, 1964). Donald Morgan's excellent *Justice William Johnson: The First Dissenter* (1954) analyzes the constitutional career of that hard-thinking, independent Jeffersonian judge and, in doing so, throws needed critical light on the inner tensions of the Marshall Court.

Carl Swisher's outstanding biography, *Roger B. Taney* (1935), relates Taney's political-economic experience and philosophy to his judicial career and, in the process, rescues the statesmanship of both the Chief Justice and his Court from the opprobrium of *Dred Scott*. Walter Lewis, *Without Fear or Favor: A Biography of Chief Justice Roger Brooke Taney* (1965) supplements Swisher by concentrating on the personal and human side of the Chief Justice. Two excellent short essays on Taney are Swisher's "Mr. Chief Justice Taney," in Dunham and Kurland (eds.), *Mr. Justice*, and Robert J. Harris, "Chief Justice Taney: Prophet of Reform and Reaction," 10 *Vanderbilt Law Review* (February, 1957). Henry G. Connor, *John Archibald Campbell* (1920) and John P. Frank, *Justice Daniel Dissenting: A Biography of Peter V. Daniel, 1784–1860* (1964) deal with the most persistent agrarians on the Court. The latter has some especially useful things to say about the composition and nature of the moderately nationalist majority of the Taney Court. That this moderate nationalism was not strictly a sectional phenomenon is clear from Francis P. Weisenburger, *The Life of John McLean* (1937) and Alexander A. Lawrence's *James Moore Wayne: Southern Unionist* (1943). Richard Leach, "Benjamin Robbins Curtis: Judicial Misfit," 25 *New England Quarterly* (December, 1952) is discerning but B. R. Curtis, Jr. (ed.), *A Memoir of Benjamin Robbins Curtis* (2 vols., 1879) remains a useful source of information on the short career of that able judge. Another approach to judicial biography—and one essential to a full understanding of the Court—is John R. Schmidhauser, "The Justices of the Supreme Court: A Collective Portrait," 3 *Midwest Journal of Political Science* (February, 1959).

THE SYNTHETIC APPROACH

Though much remains to be done (as Paul Murphy points out in "Time to Reclaim: The Current Challenge of American Constitutional History," 69 *American Historical Review* [October, 1963]), constitutional historiography has progressed significantly in quantity, sophistication, and self-awareness. One of the most important advances has been the attempt to see the Court as a part of the total legal process and to put both it and the law in the full context of American life. Charles Warren's *The Supreme Court and the Sovereign States* (1924) and Mitchell Wendell's previously noted *Relations between the Federal and State Courts* (1949) explore the judicial dimension of the federal-state relationship. Though focused on individual states, Oscar and Mary Handlin, *Commonwealth: Massachusetts, 1774–1861* (1947) and especially Louis Hartz, *Economic Policy and Democratic Thought: Pennsylvania, 1776–1860* (1948) are rich in suggestions on the political-economic-legal relationship of state and nation. The importance to American law of state courts—and the creative role played by a great state judge—is the subject of Leonard Levy, *Law of the Commonwealth and Chief Justice Shaw* (1957). John T. Horton's *James Kent: A Study in Conservatism, 1763–1847* (1939) is also valuable, though somewhat less to the point. Stanley Kutler's "John Bannister Gibson: Judicial Restraint and the Positive State," 14 *Journal of Public Law* (No. 1, 1965) deals with yet another of the great state judges who shaped the contours of American law in the formative period.

Legal education and lawyers are pertinent subjects in developing the total view. Charles Warren's *History of the Harvard Law*

School and Early American Legal Conditions in America (3 vols., 1908) is not only a history of the most important law school in the antebellum period but, as the title indicates, an account of larger legal developments. Warren's *A History of the American Bar* (1912) is also still standard. Roscoe Pound's *The Lawyer from Antiquity to Modern Times* (1953) is useful in supplying the large historical perspective. Anton-Hermann Chroust, *The Rise of the Legal Profession in America* (2 vols., 1965), though somewhat wanting in analysis, is a mine of information on the colonial and early national periods. The impact of one great lawyer on the development of the Constitution is explored in Maurice Baxter's *Daniel Webster and the Supreme Court* (1967). The broker role of Daniel Webster between the professional-economic elite and the Court is discussed in R. Kent Newmyer, "Daniel Webster as Tocqueville's Lawyer," 11 *American Journal of Legal History* (April, 1967). Harr's previously cited collection, *The Golden Age of American Law,* contains revealing contemporary statements on both legal education and the legal profession.

As yet there is no history of American law (and there will be none until a vast amount of spade work on the state and local level is done). However, Roscoe Pound, *Formative Era of American Law* (1938) throws valuable interpretive light on the main features of antebellum jurisprudence. Francis Aumann, *The Changing American Legal System: Some Selected Phases* (1940) supplies information pertinent to a larger view. One phase of the relationship between law and intellectual history is explored in Benjamin F. Wright, *American Interpretations of Natural Law* (1931) and Charles G. Haines, *The Revival of Natural Law Concepts* (1930). Max Lerner, "Constitution and Court as Symbols," 46 *Yale Law Journal* (June, 1937) and Ralph Henry Gabriel, "Constitutional Democracy: A Nineteenth-Century Faith," in Conyers Read (ed.), *The Constitution Reconsidered* (1938), both deal with a crucial extra-legal facet of constitutional history. And, finally, standing above all other efforts to relate American law to national life and indispensable for understanding the Marshall-Taney period are Willard Hurst, *Law and the Conditions of Freedom in the Nineteenth-Century United States* (1956) and Perry Miller's brilliant chapters on the legal mind in his *The Life of the Mind in America from the Revolution to the Civil War* (1965).

Glossary of Legal Terms

certiorari: a discretionary writ from a superior court calling the action of an inferior court (or a quasi-judicial body) up for review.

comity: the informal and voluntary recognition by courts of one jurisdiction of the laws and judicial decisions of another.

common law: the body of law developed and administered in England as distinguished from Civil or Roman law; also, the law derived from ancient usage and custom and judicial decisions as distinct from legislative or statute law; also, the law administered in courts of common law as distinguished from that in courts of equity.

decisional law: law determined by reference to the reported decisions of the courts.

eminent domain: power to take private property for public use.

equity: a system of jurisprudence, distinct from the common law, and affording remedial justice not available in common law courts.

habeas corpus: a writ directed to a person detaining another, commanding him to produce that person and show legal justification for the detention.

judicial review: power of the Supreme Court to negate acts of Congress that conflict with the Constitution and to overrule acts of state legislatures at variance with either the Constitution or federal laws.

libel: in practice, a written statement by a plaintiff of his cause of action and of the relief he seeks to obtain in his suit.

mandamus: a writ issued from a court of competent jurisdiction commanding the performance of a particular act specified therein.

obiter dictum: an opinion expressed by a court on some question of law which is not necessary to the decision of the case being considered.

on the merits: the inherent justice of the defendant's contention as distinguished from technical matters such as jurisdiction or pleading.

party of record: party to a legal action whose name appears on the record of the court.

plenary: full, unqualified.

private law: the law administered between citizen and citizen.

public law: that branch of law concerned with the state in its political and sovereign capacity.

quo warranto: writ by which the government commences a legal action to recover an office or franchise from a person or corporation in possession of it.

remand: to send back.

salvage: in maritime law, compensation allowed to persons by whose assistance a ship or its cargo is rescued from impending danger or recovered in cases of shipwreck.

seriatim: separately; one by one.

stare decisis: doctrine of following rules or principles laid down in previous judicial decisions, where the facts permit.

sub silentio: under silence; without notice being given.

tort: any wrongful act (not involving a breach of contract) for which a civil action may be brought; a civil wrong independent of contract.

ultra vires: beyond the scope or in excess of legal power or authority.

writ of error: a writ issued from an appellate to an inferior court commanding that the record of a case be sent up for review of an alleged error in law of the inferior court.

JUSTICES OF THE SUPREME COURT, 1801–1864

Period of Appointment

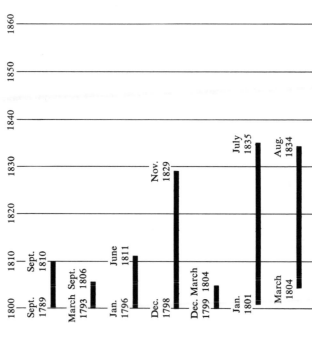

William Cushing (1732–1810), Mass., Fed.,
App. by Washington, Sept. 24, 1789

William Paterson (1745–1806), N.J., Fed.,
App. by Washington, March 4, 1793

Samuel Chase (1741–1811), Md., Fed.,
App. by Washington, Jan. 26, 1796

Bushrod Washington (1762–1829), Va., Fed.,
App. by Adams, Sept. 29, 1798

Alfred Moore (1755–1810), N.C., Fed.,
App. by Adams, Oct. 20, 1799

Chief Justice John Marshall (1755–1835),
Va., Fed., App. by Adams, Jan. 20, 1801

William Johnson (1771–1834), S.C., Rep.,
App. by Jefferson, March 22, 1804

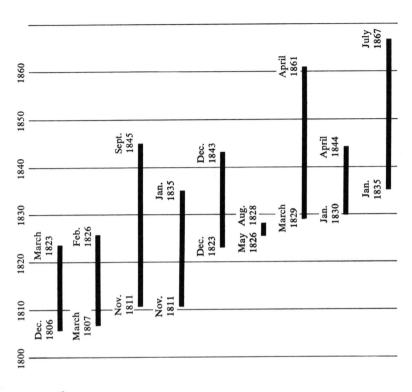

1800   1810   1820   1830   1840   1850   1860

Dec. 1806 — March 1823

Feb. 1826
March 1807

Nov. 1811 — Sept. 1845

Jan. 1835
Nov. 1811

Dec. 1823 — Dec. 1843

May Aug.
1826 1828

March 1829 — April 1861

Jan. 1830 — April 1844

Jan. 1835 — July 1867

Henry Brockholst Livingston (1757–1823),
N.Y., Rep., App. by Jefferson, Nov. 10, 1806

Thomas Todd (1765–1826), Ky., Rep.,
App. by Jefferson, Feb. 28, 1807

Joseph Story (1779–1845), Mass., Rep.,
App. by Madison, Nov. 15, 1811

Gabriel Duval (1752–1844), Md., Rep.,
App. by Madison, Nov. 15, 1811

Smith Thompson (1768–1843), N.Y., Rep.,
App. by Monroe, Sept. 1, 1823

Robert Trimble (1777–1828), Ky., Rep.,
App. by J. Q. Adams, April 11, 1826

John McLean (1785–1861), Ohio, Dem. (later
Rep.), App. by Jackson, March 6, 1829

Henry Baldwin (1780–1844), Pa., Dem.,
App. by Jackson, Jan. 4, 1830

James Moore Wayne (1790–1867), Ga., Dem.,
App. by Jackson, Jan. 7, 1835

JUSTICES OF THE SUPREME COURT, 1801–1864

Period of Appointment

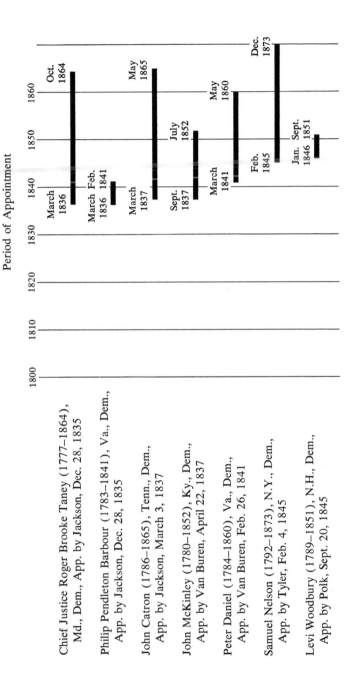

Chief Justice Roger Brooke Taney (1777–1864),
Md., Dem., App. by Jackson, Dec. 28, 1835

Philip Pendleton Barbour (1783–1841), Va., Dem.,
App. by Jackson, Dec. 28, 1835

John Catron (1786–1865), Tenn., Dem.,
App. by Jackson, March 3, 1837

John McKinley (1780–1852), Ky., Dem.,
App. by Van Buren, April 22, 1837

Peter Daniel (1784–1860), Va., Dem.,
App. by Van Buren, Feb. 26, 1841

Samuel Nelson (1792–1873), N.Y., Dem.,
App. by Tyler, Feb. 4, 1845

Levi Woodbury (1789–1851), N.H., Dem.,
App. by Polk, Sept. 20, 1845

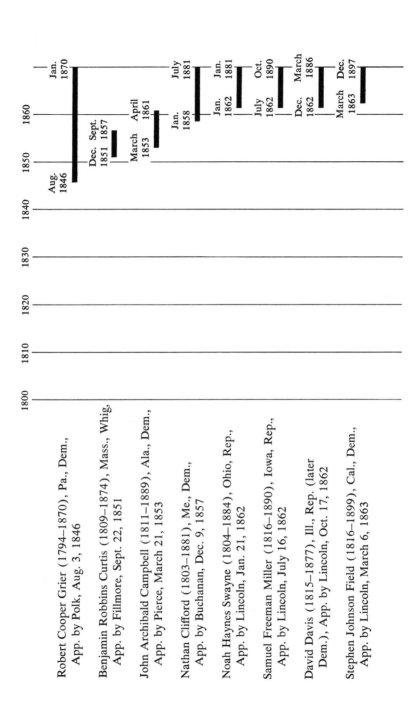

1800   1810   1820   1830   1840   1850   1860   1870

Robert Cooper Grier (1794–1870), Pa., Dem.,
App. by Polk, Aug. 3, 1846

Benjamin Robbins Curtis (1809–1874), Mass., Whig,
App. by Fillmore, Sept. 22, 1851

John Archibald Campbell (1811–1889), Ala., Dem.,
App. by Pierce, March 21, 1853

Nathan Clifford (1803–1881), Me., Dem.,
App. by Buchanan, Dec. 9, 1857

Noah Haynes Swayne (1804–1884), Ohio, Rep.,
App. by Lincoln, Jan. 21, 1862

Samuel Freeman Miller (1816–1890), Iowa, Rep.,
App. by Lincoln, July 16, 1862

David Davis (1815–1877), Ill., Rep. (later
Dem.), App. by Lincoln, Oct. 17, 1862

Stephen Johnson Field (1816–1899), Cal., Dem.,
App. by Lincoln, March 6, 1863

INDEX OF CASES

INDEX